HE IS ABLE

John Kitchen

journeyforth®
Greenville, South Carolina

Library of Congress Cataloging-in Publication Data
Names: Kitchen, John A. (John Arthur), author.
Title: He is able : you can't but God can / John A. Kitchen.
Description: Greenville, South Carolina : JourneyForth, [2019] | Includes bibliographical references.
Identifiers: LCCN 2019004914 (print) | LCCN 2019010952 (ebook) | ISBN 9781628567175 (e-book) | ISBN 9781628567168 (pbk. : alk. paper)
Subjects: LCSH: Christian life. | God (Christianity)—Faithfulness.
Classification: LCC BV4501.3 (ebook) | LCC BV4501.3 .K5735 2019 (print) | DDC 231.7—dc23
LC record available at https://lccn.loc.gov/2019004914

Design by Kristen Carruthers
Page layout by Michael Boone

Greenville, South Carolina 29609
JourneyForth Books is a division of BJU Press.

Printed in the United States of America

ISBN 978-1-62856-716-8
eISBN 978-1-62856-717-5

15 14 13 12 11 10 9 8 7 6 5 4 3 2 1

To the rising generation

One generation shall commend your works to another,
and shall declare your mighty acts.
Psalm 145:4

May you
aim for God's glory,
live in God's grace,
and move in God's power.

CONTENTS

PROLOGUE

MY DILEMMA

May I be candid? I figure we might as well be honest right up front: *I can't do it.*

I can't.

I can't be the man I ought to be. I can't be the man people expect me to be. I can't be the man I want to be. I can't be the man my family deserves.

I can't do it.

I can't be strong enough. I can't be wise enough or smart enough. I can't know enough, study enough, read widely enough, be intelligent enough.

I can't be holy, compassionate, or hopeful. I can't be faithful, humble, gentle, loving, or joyful. I can't be peaceful, patient, good, or self-controlled.

I can't stop.

I can't even start!

I can't understand it, figure it out, trace it out, or search it out.

I can't love my wife as Christ loved the church. I can't make my children love God. I can't make them want God. I can't make them walk with God.

I can't overcome the world. I can't control my own sinful impulses. I can't reign in my thoughts, corral my anxieties, or wrestle my worries into submission.

I can't answer your questions. I can't even answer *my* questions.

I can't keep it up, stay the course, or win the day. I can't find the path. I can't walk the path, even if I do find it.

I can't hang on. I can't keep going. I can't persevere to the end.

I can't figure it out, reason it through, or find my way.

I can't prolong my life. I can't guarantee myself another heartbeat, assure myself of another breath, or sustain my brain waves another second.

I can't pay God back. I can't pay God off. I can't remove my sins, pay for my sins, or destroy my sins.

I can't change my body, my face, or my hair (or lack of thereof).

I can't change my history.

I can't change my family.

I can't make my life count, discover my destiny, make a name, or leave a legacy. I can't discover, change, or attain my destiny.

I can't rise above, overcome, or triumph.

I can't be the son I ought to be. I can't be the brother I ought to be, the nephew I ought to be, the uncle I ought to be. I can't be the son-in-law or brother-in-law I ought to be.

I can't be what I want to be. I can't be what I ought to be. I can't be what I must be.

I can't justify my own existence.

I guess what I'm trying to tell you is this: *I can't!*

And, frankly, it makes me angry.

I must.

But I can't.

And I'm mad about it.

I'm angry with myself. *What's the matter with me?*

I'm angry at anyone or anything that exposes my inability. *Get out of my face!*

Yet I must. The obligation itself exposes my powerlessness and pride.

PART ONE

I CAN'T, BUT GOD CAN!

I do not understand my own actions. . . .
I do the very thing I hate. . . .
Who will deliver me from this body of death?
Thanks be to God through Jesus Christ our Lord!

Romans 7:15, 24–25

1

OUR DILEMMA

OK, I realize that was a little heavy. Not exactly the way to start a book—especially one meant to encourage.

But I took the risk because I know that in all this I am not alone. You know what I'm talking about. Don't you? *My* dilemma is *our* dilemma.

And it's not just you and me. Someone else knows this plight too, someone pretty high profile.

In a backward sort of way, that *is* encouraging.

The apostle Paul knew our frustration, anger, and angst.

> *I do not understand my own actions. For I do not do what I want, but I do the very thing I hate.* Now if *I do what I do not want,* I agree with the law, that it is good. So now it is no longer I who do it, but sin that dwells within me. For I know that *nothing good dwells in me*, that is, in my flesh. For *I have* the desire to do what is right, but *not the ability* to carry it out. For *I do not do the good I want*, but *the evil I do not want is what I keep on doing.* Now if *I do what I do not want,* it is no longer I who do it, but sin that dwells within me. So I find it to be a law that when *I want to do right,* evil lies close at hand. For I delight in the law of God, in my inner being, but *I see in my members another law waging war* against the law of my mind and making me captive to the law of

> sin that dwells in my members. *Wretched man that I am!* Who will deliver me from this body of death? (Rom. 7:15–24)

That's right. The great apostle himself had to admit, "I want to, . . . but I can't."

I hate to break the news to you: neither can you.

The apostles James and John, when asked by Jesus if they would be able to drink the cup which He must drink (i.e., suffering), eagerly replied, "We are able" (Matt. 20:22). We have to agree with the one who said, "No more naïve words have ever been spoken."[1] Jesus later would make a point to drive this home, warning, "Apart from me you can do nothing" (John 15:5).

This stands in direct contradiction to the survival instincts imbedded within the rebellious human heart. To admit *I can't* is tantamount to giving way to despair. I'm all I've got. If I can't, I'm lost!

I can't. You can't. Yet the world repeatedly, doggedly, to the death demands, *you can*!

Think of the average interview with an athletic superstar. His team has just won the coveted world championship. The confetti is still falling around him. The champagne spray creates rainbows under the glare of fame's bright lights. The world's populace has logged on and tuned in by the hundreds of millions. His sweaty brow sports the freshly minted championship cap, cocked sideways on his head. He hugs the trophy that signifies the ultimate triumph in his chosen profession. A reporter shoves a microphone into his emotion-laden face and asks, "How did you get here?" The answer is as predictable as tomorrow's sunrise: "I just believed in myself. This proves that you can do anything you set your mind to!" Cascades of cheers swallow him in congratulations as he fades into the merry mayhem.

Across the arena another sportscaster stands with another athlete. Same sport. Same tournament. Same game just concluded. Though only feet away from the applause and bright lights that adorn the victor, this sportscaster stands in a room filled with silence, save a few groans and scattered whimpers. Sitting drenched in sweat and dejection, another world-class athlete finds a microphone in his face. The question is, "Where do you go from here?" The answer: "I just have to believe in myself. I have to get my head straight and keep telling myself that I can do anything I set my mind to."

What do you make of that?

Allow me to set forth my conclusion as politely as I can: Baloney!

Which is it? Can you? Or can't you? Does just believing in yourself enable you to win or not? Did the one athlete believe in himself better or more fully than the other one?

Think of it in physical terms. Overcoming by believing in yourself is like trying to lift yourself off the ground with nothing but your own arms. It just can't work. You must have an anchor point outside of yourself and a power source capable of effecting the move.

All reality conspires both to demand *you must* and to prove *you can't.*

Can you imagine anything more futile? More exasperating? Anything more damning?

2

THE GREAT ADMISSION

Our dilemma doesn't have to give way to despair. Because of God's love and grace, *I can't* is actually the gateway to the good news. The admission *I can't* opens the door of your life to one who can. In fact, until you wholeheartedly confess *I can't*, you aren't ready to hear or respond to the gospel. The doorway to the good news requires getting low and admitting *I can't.*

Admitting *I can't* is the gateway to the good news of the gospel both for salvation of the sinner and for the sanctification of the child of God. It is the doorway through which you begin your relationship with God, and it opens to the continuance of your relationship with God. This is the gateway to salvation from the guilt of your sin before God and from a self-defined, self-energized, earth-bound, disappointing Christian experience.

What's that? You don't agree?

I submit to you that Jesus can convince you in one statement. Are you ready? Here it is: "Be perfect, as your heavenly Father is perfect" (Matt. 5:48).

Perfect.

Look perfection full in the face and answer. Will it be: *I can*? Or must it be *I can't*?

Many years ago when the earth's crust was just beginning to cool, I participated in track and field. Allow me to return to one of my main events, the high jump. It is that event in which you run toward and, unaided by anything outside your own body, propel your entire body over a bar. The bar is moved higher and higher until no one present can get his body over it. At this moment the world record for the high jump stands at just a hair's breadth over eight feet. Eight feet. Only one human in all of history has ever accomplished this.

For the sake of argument let's just suppose that the standard for "perfect" would be set at fifteen feet. A regulation basketball hoop is ten feet. Make it five feet higher than that.

Now you are brought to stand before that bar. My question is simple: Can you?

There isn't anyone in human history who can honestly answer *I can*. Every human who has ever existed has to admit, *I can't.*

Jesus said, "Be perfect, as your heavenly Father is perfect." He also warned us, "Apart from me you can do nothing" (John 15:5).

Now lay alongside Jesus' words this statement from Buddha: "He is able who thinks he is able."

I don't mean to be disrespectful, but in light of reality Buddha's statement is silliness.

Sure there are some things we can do if we really redouble our efforts and focus the strength that is ours as creatures of God. If you try really hard for several months, you might be able to lose five pounds. You could color your hair. You could quit your job and follow your dream.

But you can't add a single minute to your life. You can't give your life significance. You can't transform your basic personality.

It is the worst day of your life when you realize you can't. And yet it is also the most wonderful day of your life when you admit you can't—because that's the day you are ready to finally discover that *God can.*

3

GOD OF THE IMPOSSIBLE

You can't, but God can!

You can't be wise, but Jesus can be wisdom in you. You can't be holy, but Jesus can be holiness in and through you. You can't be faithful, always, in everything. But Jesus can be faithfulness in and through you. You can't love—not everyone, not all the time. But Jesus is able to not only give you love but to love through you. You can't change your heart, but Jesus can. You can't change your thinking, but Jesus can. You can't change your outlook, but Jesus can. You can't dispel your depression, but Jesus can. You can't overcome, but Christ already has and will, in and through you.

It is pretty simple: He is able; you aren't. You can't, but God can.

Listen to this profound statement of the truth from Major W. Ian Thomas: "I cannot—God never said I could; but *God can*, and always said He would!"[1]

This is what Jesus meant when He said, "Apart from me you can do nothing." It is what Paul was after when he said that it is "Christ in you" that is your "hope" (Col. 1:27).

Look at Jesus' assertion in its fuller context: "Abide in me, and I in you. As the branch cannot bear fruit by itself, unless it abides in the vine, neither can you, unless you abide in me. I am the vine; you are the branches. Whoever abides in me and I in him, he it is that bears much fruit, for apart from me you can do nothing" (John 15:4–5).

Go to your nearest vineyard and remove a branch from its vine. Set it aside. Come back at the end of the season. What do you have?

Death.

But take the same length of time to nurture that branch's connection to the vine and you'll have "fruit . . . more fruit . . . much fruit" (vv. 2, 5).

It is the branch's connection to the vine that makes all the difference, for the life is in the vine. The life is only in the branch as it is in abiding relationship with and connection to the vine. The life of the vine in the branch is what produces fruit.

Now here is a truly amazing fact: Jesus willingly subjected Himself to that same kind of relationship with His Father. While on earth, Jesus chose to live in relationship to the Father in precisely the same way we must now live in relationship to Him. This is why He said, "Truly, truly, I say to you, the Son can do nothing of his own accord, but only what he sees the Father doing. For whatever the Father does, that the Son does likewise" (John 5:19).

Look how often during His earthly ministry Jesus spoke of His relationship of dependence upon the Father:

> I can do nothing on my own. As I hear, I judge, and my judgment is just, because I seek not my own will but the will of him who sent me. (John 5:30)

> So Jesus said to them, "When you have lifted up the Son of Man, then you will know that I am he, and that I do nothing on my own authority, but speak just as the Father taught me." (John 8:28)

> For I have not spoken on my own authority, but the Father who sent me has himself given me a commandment—what to say and what to speak. (John 12:49)

> Do you not believe that I am in the Father and the Father is in me? The words that I say to you I do not speak on my own authority, but the Father who dwells in me does his works. (John 14:10)

And Jesus clearly established that it would be this kind of ongoing, abiding relationship that would be our pattern of life and discipleship with Him: "In that day you will know that I am in my Father, and you in me, and I in you" (John 14:20).

This is the pattern for the whole of one's Christian life! This is where one *begins* the Christian life. This is how one *continues* in the Christian life. Paul told the believers in Colossae, "As you received Christ Jesus the Lord, so walk in him" (Col. 2:6). The pattern for continuing is the same as for beginning. This is why Paul could tell the Philippian Christians, "I can do all things through him who strengthens me" (Phil. 4:13). If he had cut that short and said merely "I can do all things," his writings would be found in the self-help aisle at the bookstore. He would be considered a friend of Buddha. But the only way Paul allowed himself to say "I can" is because he knew it was "through him who strengthens me." Indeed, he told the believers in Colossae that the great mystery of the gospel is this: "Christ in you, the hope of glory" (Col. 1:27). It is only through the risen, reigning, all-powerful Christ dwelling within that anyone can honestly say, "I can."

4

LIFE! NOT BEHAVIOR MODIFICATION

Any version of the Christian life that enters through a door other than the confession *I can't* is just another kind of behavior modification. Jesus did not give Himself in order to offer behavior modification but to offer *life*! Jesus came to bring more than reformation of our actions, but to bring complete transformation of our being. Too much that passes for Christianity simply makes us more adept at managing our independence from God. It is training in how to make ourselves happy, by controlling ourselves and our environment . . . with God's help, of course.

This is sub-Christian.

Until we come to a genuine *I can't*, all preaching, teaching, and reading on the Christian life sounds like *try harder*! There is no good news in *try harder*.

So here's the basic truth about life: You can't. But there's good news: God can.

It is impossible to enter into the joy and hope and life of *God can* until you embrace and admit you can't.

You can't stop. You can't overcome, compensate, quit, or change. You can't conquer. You can't triumph. You can't refrain. You can't remain.

Need I continue?

Clearly, you can't. Otherwise you would. You would love to, but you can't.

God can. Whatever it is, God can.

OK, God is able. But when and in what is God both able *and willing*?

There are two conditions under which God's infinite ability and gracious willingness join arms. The first is this: Is it *good* for me? The second is: Is it *glorifying* to Him?

Oh, and by the way, God gets the last word on defining what is good for you and what will glorify Him.

This is not a carte blanche kind of deal. This is no blank check. God is able to do anything that He wills to do. But what is He *willing* to do?

Fortunately we are not left in the dark. The New Testament us tells repeatedly what God is able and willing to do. Here are just a few:

- God "is able to save to the uttermost those who draw near to God through him" (Heb. 7:25).
- God "is able to strengthen you according to my gospel and the preaching of Jesus Christ" (Rom. 16:25).
- God "is able to help those who are being tempted" (Heb. 2:18).
- God "is able to keep you from stumbling and to present you blameless before the presence of his glory with great joy" (Jude 1:24).
- "God is able to make all grace abound to you, so that having all sufficiency in all things at all times, you may abound in every good work" (2 Cor. 9:8).
- Abraham was "fully convinced that God was able to do what he had promised" (Rom. 4:21).
- God "is able to do far more abundantly than all that we ask or think, according to the power at work within us" (Eph. 3:20).
- Paul said, "I am not ashamed, for I know whom I have believed, and I am convinced that he is able to guard until that day what has been entrusted to me" (2 Tim. 1:12).
- Abraham "considered that God was able even to raise [Isaac] from the dead, from which, figuratively speaking, he did receive him back" (Heb. 11:19).
- "There is only one lawgiver and judge, he who is able to save and to destroy" (James 4:12).

These passages represent what God is ready to do in and through you. They describe the possibilities of a divinely generated life, the kind of life Paul lived and invited all God's children to enter into as well.

Paul said he would speak of nothing "except what Christ has accomplished through [him]" (Rom. 15:18). It is no different today. "Christ who is your life" (Col. 3:4) desires to produce His life in and through you. When recounting all his accomplishments in ministry, Paul was careful to say, "It was not I, but the grace of God that is with me" (1 Cor. 15:10). When Paul and Barnabas met with fellow believers in Jerusalem, they testified of what "God had done through them" (Acts 15:12). Again in a later meeting he shared with them "the things that God had done . . . through his ministry" (Acts 21:19). Whose ministry? Paul's. Who had performed it? God! But He had done it through Paul by means of his willing obedience.

Jesus' overcoming life flowed through a mere human being, a life lived in the flow of Jesus' own divine life. What would it take to see God do such things in and through *you*? What will it take to move from languishing in your inability to living in God's ability?

5

TENDER YOUR RESIGNATION

The first step to living in God's *can* is embracing you *can't*. We begin the transition from our inability to God's ability by getting low.

Yet *you can't* sounds so much like resignation, like giving up, like quitting.

And that is exactly what it is! Resignation.

You must tender your resignation. You must quit.

Here's my challenge to you. As soon as you close the book on this opening section, take a few moments to write a letter of resignation. Address it to God. Tell Him that you quit.

Perhaps you could say something like this: "Dear heavenly Father, I resign from trying to do it myself. I resign from trying to be Jesus. I resign from trying to make unholiness shine like holiness. I resign from working to make unrighteousness clean up and march around as righteousness. I resign from believing that if I simply try harder I will one day be able. I resign from ruling my life. I resign from reigning over my circumstances. I resign from controlling the people and circumstances of my life. I am not God. Only You are. O God, be God in me! I am simply taking my place as a worshiper, a dependent worshiper at Your feet."

Now let's be honest. We have trouble with this. We don't like to admit this. This is humiliating. It seems to dash all our hopes.

But it is essential, for as long as we insist that we can, God won't.

But before I close this section let me clarify something lest you misunderstand. You are not resigning from doing *anything*. You are resigning from doing anything *on your own*. You are tendering your notice and resigning from trying to do things in your own strength, in your own power, in your own wisdom, in your own goodness, benevolence, and love.

Weakness is the doorway that opens into the vault of God's strength. Your *can't* leads to God's *can*. Your *inability* leads to the expression of God's *ability*.

God's own word is: "My grace is sufficient for you, for my power is made perfect in weakness." Paul decided, "Therefore I will boast all the more gladly of my weaknesses, so that the power of Christ may rest upon me" (2 Cor. 12:9).

It is as true for you as it was for the great apostle.

We are about to turn our full attention to what God can do. Our focus will be on God's *can*, not your *can't*. We aren't to dwell on the negative, but we do have to admit it before we can move on.

Take some time now to write that letter to God. Tuck it away. You may need the reminder now and then. But then let's move on to set our sights on our ever able, always capable, never undone, never outgunned Savior.

Remember, He is able. You can't, but He can!

PART TWO

GOD IS ABLE TO SAVE YOU

Consequently, he is able to save to the uttermost those who draw near to God through him, since he always lives to make intercession for them.

Hebrews 7:25

6

POP QUIZ!

All right, class. Time for a pop quiz.

Please take out a sheet of paper.

I'm serious! Please take out a sheet of paper and something to write with.

This quiz will consist of four questions.

You won't need to turn this in. The results are between you and God.

First question: *On a scale of 1 to 10, how happy are you with your life?* A score of one is reserved for a life that could not possibly be more unhappy. Ten would indicate that nothing could happen to make you any happier than you are at this moment. Please record your score.

Second question: *What would it take to make your life a perfect ten?* Presuming you didn't score your life at a ten, what would have to happen for you to rate your life a perfect ten? Please write down your response.

Now, the third question: *On a scale of 1 to 10, how happy is* God *with your life?* Ah, this is a twist, isn't it? Perhaps you're not accustomed to thinking in these terms, but record your honest answer.

Finally, and perhaps you see where this is going by now: *What would it take for* God *to score your life a perfect ten?* Seriously, write your thoughts down.

What is the point of this quiz? To reveal this: Perhaps your perceived problem isn't your real problem. Maybe your professed need isn't your actual need.

Think of the guy sitting at home on Saturday evening. He's got a serious case of the munchies. He isn't so much hungry as possessed by a craving. He asks his wife what time the closest store closes.

Too late! Rats!

He inquires, "Do you want to go get some ice cream?" She doesn't. He can't stand it. He can't stop thinking about it. But somehow he makes it through the weekend.

On Monday morning he goes to a previously scheduled doctor's appointment. Tests reveal a mass growing on one of his internal organs.

Now think back to Saturday evening. What was his real need? Was it the one that had seized his attention and which he could barely shake?

Is it possible that your perceived problem isn't your real problem?

As Americans we are far more in tune with our own happiness than God's. We wrestle with questions like *What makes me happy?* and *What's at stake if things remain unchanged?* It is highly unlikely that we ask the more essential questions such as *What makes* God *happy?* And again, now with even more hanging in the balance, *What is at stake if things remained unchanged?*

This is why Americans are so unlikely to be drawn into a conversation that begins with a question like *Are you saved?* That just isn't a conversation we feel compelled to enter. Most Americans didn't wake up this morning wondering about God's pleasure. We, therefore, have little interest in statements of Scripture like that in Hebrews 7:25: "He [Jesus] is able to save."

The average American hears that kind of verse like they might hear the guy who says, "I can juggle four running chainsaws all at the same time!"

"OK, I didn't wake up this morning thinking, 'I wonder if any living person can juggle four running chainsaws at the same time. But, go ahead, if you feel the need to.' "

We just aren't all that interested in death, eternity, and salvation. Maybe we'll listen as a novelty, for a moment, out of curiosity or courtesy. But we're not likely to listen with any sense of gravity or vital concern on a personal level.

7

THE ANSWER FOR A FAILING SCORE

So how'd you score on our pop quiz?

If it's left you a bit disconcerted, that's not a bad thing. The Bible clearly tells us that "the wrath of God is [right now, actively, in the present, being] revealed from heaven against all ungodliness and unrighteousness of men, who by their unrighteousness suppress the truth" (Rom. 1:18). The world may conceal the fact, but "there is only one lawgiver and judge, he who is able to save and to destroy" (James 4:12). Jesus warned, "Do not fear those who kill the body but cannot kill the soul. Rather fear him who can destroy both soul and body in hell" (Matt. 10:28). Indeed, "It is a terrifying thing to fall into the hands of the living God" (Heb. 10:31, NASB).

I know this has gotten pretty intense pretty quickly, but two things are vitally important for all of us to see. First, *my* perceived problem may not be *my* most acute problem. Second, the solution to that most acute problem is not to be found within me.

In the light of this dilemma consider this simple line of Scripture and the good news it provides: "Consequently, he is able to save to the uttermost those who draw near to God through him, since he always lives to make intercession for them" (Heb. 7:25).

The "he" being referred to is Jesus Christ. Jesus "is able to save."

Save? From what?

Great question! It really is, for this is precisely where we begin to go askew in our thinking.

If we apply this statement to our default question of *Am I happy?*, we will probably view Jesus as a lifestyle upgrade. You'll consider those things that stand in the way of your life being the perfect ten you dream of, and you'll hear "He is able to save" as a promise that Jesus will overcome all those threats and make you ultimately happy.

In such a case, Jesus is just another app. Your marriage got you down? Jesus is the app for that. Is your health getting in the way of your dream? Jesus is the app for that. Your finances keeping you from the life you want to have? Jesus is the app for that.

If you view this promise of Jesus' saving ability in that light, I can assure you that you will eventually be disappointed. This will not be because Jesus is unable to do all the things on your list, but because that wasn't His mission and those aren't His promises.

If you view this promise of God and demand that Jesus give you the spouse you've always dreamed of, that house you've pictured in your mind, the radically obedient, healthy, joy-giving children, the job, the health, the time to enjoy it all . . . well, you'll be disappointed. And it's not because Jesus is against those things.

But if you apply this grand promise to life's most essential question—*Is God happy with me and my life?*—you may be ready to view Jesus as a true Savior.

As it is in our natural state, we're trying to live life in God's world without God. This brings God's displeasure, judgment, and wrath. Jesus can take you from such a dire position before an infinitely holy and powerful God and bring you into a place where you stand in His favor, blessing, and love.

Do you remember the story of the guy who had it all, but still knew he was missing something? "And Jesus said to His disciples, 'Truly I say to you, it is hard for a rich man [read: the man with everything in place for his happiness] to enter the kingdom of heaven. Again I say to you, it is easier for a camel to go through the eye of a needle, than for a rich man [the man who has achieved earthly happiness] to enter the kingdom of God.' When the disciples heard this, they were very astonished and said, 'Then who can be saved?' And looking at them Jesus said to them, 'With people this is impossible, but with God all things are possible' " (Matt. 19:23–26, NASB).

Jesus *is able*. That is to say He has the capacity, power, and ability to do what you can never do—make God happy.

Did you get that? Jesus is able to make God happy with you.

You can't—not through any amount of reform, not through any accumulation of righteous works, not through any amount of devotion to religion.

You can't. But Jesus can. He is able!

And Jesus is not just able, but able "to the uttermost."

Most hear "save" as related to God intervening to make life happy for us. We hear, "Jesus will save me from anything that would rob me of my dream!" Not surprisingly, many then turn away from Him because He didn't perform as required for their happiness. They ask with venom in their voices, "Where was God when __________?"

But the promise of Jesus' saving power is not applied to our list of threats to our happiness. It is to be applied to God's list of possible threats to His happiness with us.

Ponder that.

Jesus is fully able to save you from the things that would make God continue in His unhappiness with you.

8

TO THE MAX

The promise is Jesus "is able to save to the uttermost." Maybe we could say, Jesus "is able to save" *to the max*. It's a legitimate thought because the word translated "uttermost" can refer both to *time* and to *scope*.

As it relates to time, it is sometimes translated "He is able also to save forever" (Heb. 7:25 NASB). In this sense it is promising that there will never be a time throughout all eternity when anything could ever arise to make God displeased with you. No event in life, no accusation at the judgment seat, nothing in the ten millionth year of existence in the new heavens and new earth.

Nothing! Ever!

As it relates to scope, it might be translated "he is able to save to the uttermost." There will never be anything—no enemy, no accusation, no amount of persecution, no loss, no gain, no power of hell, no calamity, no disease, no accident, no incident, no person, no circumstance—that "will be able to separate us from the love of God in Christ Jesus our Lord" (Rom. 8:39).

This speaks a wonderful word to you if you are among the unbelieving ones. It also speaks a great message to you if you are among those who believe and yet have labored under a deep, but perhaps unspoken, uncertainty about God's love. Do you lack assurance of your salvation?

Here is John Owen's wise counsel:

> Men are afraid to have good thoughts of God. They think it is a boldness to eye God as good, gracious, tender, kind, loving.

> I speak of saints. They can judge him hard, austere, severe, almost implacable, and fierce (the very worst affections of the very worst of men, and most hated by God). Is not this soul-deceit from Satan? Was it not his design from the beginning to inject such thoughts of God? Assure yourself, then, there is nothing more acceptable to the Father than for us to keep up our hearts unto him as the eternal fountain of all that rich grace which flows out to sinners in the blood of Jesus.[1]

Hear it again. Hear it well: Jesus "is able to save to the *uttermost*"!

But, why, may I ask, is Jesus "able" to do this?

It is because "he always lives to make intercession for them."

Is this not our great need?

In the midst of his suffering Job knew this as his greatest necessity. He said God "is not a man, as I am, that I might answer him, that we should come to trial together. There is no arbiter between us, who might lay his hand on us both" (Job 9:32–33).

My greatest need is for someone to stand between this utterly holy God whose wrath rightly rests upon me in my natural state, and me, who stands in danger of His judgment of my sins.

9

A GAPPER

A gapper: one who stands between; one in the middle; one who can look both directions, reach both parties, and bridge the divide.

That is our great need. We need a gapper.

The Bible's word for such a one is *priest*. A priest is one who represents man to God and God to man. He stands between heaven and earth, between God and man. And this is precisely what the writer of Hebrews has been talking about for some time now.

The Old Covenant, handed down by God through Moses, made provision for priests. They were from the family of Aaron, descended through Levi's tribe. These priests "were many in number, because they were prevented by death from continuing in office" (Hebrews 7:23).

That is to say that those priests were *temporary* (in that they were mortal and eventually died), *fallible* (bearing their own failures and sins), *many* (for they had to be continuously replaced), *shadowy* (for their sacrifices were but the outline of the true sacrifice to come), and *repetitive* (for those sacrifices had to be offered again and again, being ineffectual in actually changing the worshiper's standing with God).

But under the New Covenant, Jesus has become a superior priest. He is our High Priest. He came not from the tribe of Levi or from Aaron's family. Rather, He came after the order of a priest described only briefly in the Old Testament. Of Him, God the Father said, "You are a priest forever, after the order of Melchizedek" (v. 17).

The Bible provides no genealogy for Melchizedek. He simply appears upon the scene. Nor are we told of his death; he simply fades from the spotlight. He was a human being, a shadowy prefiguring of the one to come who would perfectly be both God and man. As such, Christ is truly the king of righteousness (v. 2), the king who makes peace between God and man (v. 2). He truly had no beginning (v. 3), being the eternal Son of God incarnate. He has no ending (v. 3), for though He died (as the sacrifice for our sins) He is alive forevermore in the power of "an indestructible life" (v. 16)!

The priests of Aaron's line passed away, not only because they died one after another, but because their entire order has been replaced by a better Priest. They were temporary, but Jesus is *permanent* (for He is immortal; He died, but rose again, never again to die). The old priests were fallible, but Jesus is *perfect* (without sin of His own). They were many, but He is *singular* (unique, irreplaceable, enduring, eternal, and sufficient as one who lives forever). Those priests were a mere shadow, but Jesus is the substance that cast that shadow (the long prophesied reality). They offered sacrifices that had to be repeated, but the sacrifice of this High Priest is perpetual (offered and accepted by the Father "once for all") (v. 27).

> For it was indeed fitting that we should have such a high priest, holy, innocent, unstained, separated from sinners, and exalted above the heavens. He has no need, like those high priests, to offer sacrifices daily, first for his own sins and then for those of the people, since he did this once for all when he offered up himself. For the law appoints men in their weakness as high priests, but the word of the oath, which came later than the law, appoints a Son who has been made perfect forever. (Heb. 7:26–28)

Remember where Jesus said the Father's standard has been set? "Be perfect, as your heavenly Father is perfect" (Matt. 5:48). Who among us is able to be perfect? You can't. I can't. But Jesus is "perfect forever" (Heb. 7:28)!

Do you see? Job's cry has been answered in the person of Jesus Christ, our High Priest. Thus the apostle John can declare, "My little children, I am writing these things to you so that you may not sin. But if anyone does sin, *we have an advocate* with the Father, Jesus Christ the righteous" (1 John 2:1). The apostle Paul asks, "Who is to condemn?" Who will ever arise to bring a condemning accusation against the one for whom Jesus serves as High Priest? He is chagrined by the very thought! No! He asserts, "Christ Jesus is the one who died—more than that, who was raised—who is at the right hand of God, who indeed *is interceding for us*" (Rom. 8:34)!

When it is said that Jesus makes intercession for us, don't picture a loving Jesus begging an angry Father not to unleash His wrath upon us.

Though assuredly imperfect, I think the following picture is closer to reality. Picture word of some sin you've committed rising up against you at the Father's throne. All of heaven gasps at the awareness. The eyes of countless holy ones turn toward the throne to see the Father's response. But no countenance of anger or expression of holy horror is found. Rather He turns to His right and casts a glance to the one sitting enthroned there. He catches the eye of his Son, Jesus, our High Priest. The two exchange a knowing glance that says, "This too was covered by my death upon the cross; this one also was judged there already, and nothing can bring it back upon this child of yours." Satisfied, the Father turns His gaze back upon you as a smile plays out across His holy countenance and a word of command releases fresh rivers of divine love, forgiveness, grace, and mercy that envelope you one more time.

This, my friend, will be the scene throughout all this life and throughout all eternity. No matter what. No matter what you do. No matter what you fail to do. No matter what anyone else ever does or fails to do.

With His last gasps of earthly breath Jesus said, "It is finished" (John 19:30). And indeed it is. "This makes Jesus the guarantor of a better covenant" (Heb. 7:22).

Here then is what we must rest in by faith. Read it aloud. Make it more than a recitation; make it a declaration: *My eternal salvation depends not upon me, but upon an eternal Savior making eternal intercession on my behalf.*

With an everlasting Savior making eternal intercession which can never fail or end, what again is it that threatens you?

Fanny Crosby got it absolutely correct; this is a "blessed assurance." Through "perfect submission" we soon enough find that "all is at rest." You can truly sing, "I [when found by faith] in my Savior am happy and blest." When God is happy, then I find my happiness! Whatever may come, you can be found "watching and waiting, looking above, filled with His goodness, lost in His love."[1]

10

FOR ME?

But let us be equally clear, as is the writer of the scriptural promise, this is not the experience of everyone. I must ask, does Jesus thus pray for *you*?

It is a legitimate question, for He only makes such intercession for "those who draw near to God through him" (Heb. 7:25).

To "draw near to God" (v. 19) is our great need and God's great goal—restoring us to fellowship with Him. It is precisely this which the writer of Hebrews is occupied with throughout the letter.

> Since then we have a great high priest who has passed through the heavens, Jesus, the Son of God, . . . *Let us* then with confidence *draw near* to the throne of grace, that we may receive mercy and find grace to help in time of need. (Heb 4:14, 16)

> Therefore, brothers, since we have confidence to enter the holy places by the blood of Jesus, by the new and living way that he opened for us through the curtain, that is, through his flesh, and since we have a great priest over the house of God, *let us draw near* with a true heart in full assurance of faith, with our hearts sprinkled clean from an evil conscience and our bodies washed with pure water. (Heb 10:19–22)

> And without faith it is impossible to please him, for whoever would *draw near* to God must believe that he exists and that he rewards those who seek him. (Heb. 11:6)

God wants you near Him. For it is there He can give to you a heart that can be cleansed from guilt (Heb. 10:22), His assurance of welcome and forgiveness (vv. 19–22), His mercy and grace to help when you are in need, and reward as you seek fellowship with Him (11:6).

Don't you see? God rescues you not simply to save Himself the hassle of judging you, but to shower you with His lavish grace and goodness.

I wonder if a mental picture would help us here.

Imagine a time when you've failed to obey your earthly father, but you approach him with your confession of wrongdoing. What response meets you? Which one of these scenes more accurately portrays the heavenly Father's response as you draw near to Him through Christ? A father who yells, "Get out of here! I don't have to mess with you!" Or one who opens his arms and invites you, "Come here, my child. I'm so glad you came. I could tell there was something between us, and it's been eating at me."

Jesus told us, "No one can come to me unless the Father who sent me draws him" (John 6:44).

Listen carefully to me: The Father has chosen you to hear the call of the gospel today. He has steered your attention to the words on these pages. It is no accident. In so doing He is drawing you to Jesus. He promised that "all that the Father gives me will come to me, and whoever comes to me I will never cast out" (John 6:37).

Your Father is calling you . . . to Himself . . . into His love . . . to share in His life. Right here; right now. You can come with confidence through Jesus, knowing that when you come you will never be turned away and never cast out.

I feel it incumbent upon me, however, to be very clear about what it means to "draw near to God."

You must do this *personally*. I can't do this for you, nor can your parents, your friend, your pastor, or any earthly priest. You must personally come to God through faith in Christ. The verb in the original Greek text of the New Testament is in the middle voice, emphasizing that while the Father must draw you, you must make a decision.

Additionally, you must do this *perpetually*. What does that mean? It means you must draw near to God through Christ, not just for a moment, but as an enduring lifestyle. That same verb is in the present tense, emphasizing this is not a one-and-done approach. We might translate it this way: "those who draw near and keep on drawing near to God through him."

God is looking not just to elicit a response from you (though every life—earthly and heavenly, temporal and eternal—begins at a moment in time), but for an enduring relationship in which you come and keep on coming to God through Jesus.

Our journey which began with questions now ends with two more.

- Have you come to God through Jesus Christ for salvation?
- Are you daily, moment by moment, drawing near to God through Christ for His ongoing, present work of salvation in your life?

PART THREE

GOD IS ABLE TO ESTABLISH YOU

Now to him who is able to strengthen you according to my gospel and the preaching of Jesus Christ, according to the revelation of the mystery that was kept secret for long ages.

Romans 16:25

11

GROUNDED AND FOUNDED

We've been gazing upon God's saving ability as if viewing a monitor being fed from security cameras placed at the throne of God. Jesus "is able to save to the uttermost those who draw near to God through him, since he always lives to make intercession for them" (Heb. 7:25). Our eternal salvation rests upon an eternal Savior making eternal intercession on our behalf.

That's the scene as it is in heaven—this very moment.

What, I wonder, does that same grace look like as it operates down here upon the earth? How does that show up for you in your workplace, bedroom, or school?

Before I *state* the answer, let me *show* you the answer.

When I was a kid, I loved helping my dad set new fence posts. The joy wasn't in the digging of post holes. That, frankly, wasn't much fun at all. If you've ever had that "pleasure" you know what I mean.

No, for me the fun started once we dropped the post into the newly dug hole. After getting it plumb, one of us held the post, while the other gradually filled dirt back into the hole, stopping to tamp down the dirt around the post with the end of the shovel handle or a long stick.

More dirt. More tamping. Repeat both as necessary. Eventually the hole was filled.

Then joy made its entrance. I'd take hold of the post and try to rock it back and forth. I was administering the wobble test. But finding that post rock solid, stable, immovable was sheer delight to this young boy. For some strange reason (psychoanalyze me, if you like) that was to me deeply satisfying.

Now compare that to Mackinac Bridge, which spans the waters that join Lake Superior and Lake Michigan, connecting lower and upper Michigan. In total the bridge is five miles in length. The roadway hangs some two hundred feet above the water. Those who constructed the bridge worked without safety nets or harnesses. Five men lost their lives during its construction.

The bridge faces several threats. High winds are the first great danger. Gales in excess of seventy miles per hour are known to sweep across the straits of Mackinac. In 1989 Leslie Ann Pluhar was driving her Yugo across the bridge when a gust of wind swept her car over the three-foot-high side railing, plunging her to her death. The bridge is actually constructed to sway as much as thirty-five feet from side to side in order to endure the winds. A second threat is the deep waters into which the bridge is set, up to 295 feet deep at mid-span. The final threat is ice buildup during the deep freeze of winter and the pressure the ice places upon the bridge's supporting structures.

Yet for all these threats, the pilings of the bridge are fixed. Some 200,000 tons of concrete was used in its construction. The bridge rests upon massive concrete piers—the largest ever struck in suspension bridge construction—submerged to depths up to 203 feet into the earth.

What do these illustrations have to do with what God is able to do in the life of one He has saved and brought into relationship with Himself through Jesus?

As the apostle Paul closed the book of Romans, his spirit and pen soared into benediction. With eyes full of God, Paul marked what He alone is able to do: "Now to him who is able to strengthen you . . ." (16:25).

The word "strengthen" is a legitimate translation of the corresponding Greek verb. But "strengthen" strikes me as rather vague. I prefer the word chosen by a number of other translations: "Now to Him who is able to *establish* you . . ." (NASB, NKJV).

It is God's intent not only to save you, but to "establish" you in that salvation. The Greek verb means "setting up something so that it remains immovable."[1] It points to strengthening, making firm, fixing in place, or, as I am suggesting, *establishing* something.

Remember George Bailey in the classic Christmas film *It's a Wonderful Life*? Every time George charges up the stairs of his family's old home, the wooden knob atop the bottom post of their banister comes off in his hand. In frustration he raises the knob with an inclination to slam it back into place. But he reins in his anger and gently places it back upon its post, albeit with a dramatic display of self-control.

Have you ever wondered why Frank Capra inserted that repeated bit into the film? I think it's a parable of what George's life had become—flimsy, unstable, rickety, falling apart, and being held together only by the greatest exertion of his energies. George labored with all his might over all those years just to keep the Building and Loan solvent. And just like the wooden knob atop his banister post (and the rest of George's life as well), it was constantly ready to fall apart.

Sound like anyone you know?

12

GOSPEL GROUNDED

Have you ever been talking with your spouse or a friend while browsing through a department store, only to lift your head and realize they've abandoned you and roamed off to other parts of the store? Inevitably there's some stranger staring back at you with wide eyes betraying a hint of fear.

Me too.

It is a reminder of how vital it is to know whether you're in the right conversation. So let's make certain we're both on the same page: I am speaking to those who claim faith in Jesus Christ.

Is that you?

If you're not sure, you may want to revisit section one before moving on. If you are confident the answer is yes, then let me share some more good news.

God has set you to *rest* upon the finished work of Christ. Your whole weight for this life and eternity is placed upon what God has proven able to do through Christ. His invitation—indeed, His command—is that you *rest* there, in faith.

Wonderful news! As you contemplate what God has proven able to do for you, exhale demonstrably, just as an expression of praise to God. *Rest!*

As you soak in the glow of this good news, let me say that the news gets even better. The moment you transfer your trust from yourself (or whatever or whomever else you may have placed it upon) to Jesus, He immediately goes to work to establish you immovable in that place of rest.

How does God establish us as His children in the gospel? Amazingly enough He does so by the gospel!

Huh?

Here's how Paul puts it: "Now to Him who is able to establish you *according to my gospel*" (Rom. 16:25 NKJV).

The entire letter to the Romans is really an extended explanation of the gospel. Paul began with the gospel (1:16–17) and, having unfolded, expounded, and explained the gospel, it is with the gospel that he ends (16:25).

So may we ask without sounding pedantic, what is the gospel?

The gospel, as the book of Romans (along with the rest of the Scriptures) tells us, is that all people everywhere are born under sin, separated from God, and doomed to face His wrath. Yet by God's grace, the debt of sin has been paid, the penalty of sin endured, and the power of sin broken by Jesus Christ at the cross. But there is more! Just as all your sins were credited to Christ at the cross (and thus He died in your place), so all His righteousness is credited to you. It is yours simply through repentant faith. Thus you are welcomed by the Father and have life that will outlive this life. All of this is available to you not on the basis of your religious or moral performance, but as a gift, received through faith.

That is the gospel—in a nutshell.

Look at that elaboration of the gospel again. What do you see?

Don't see the gospel simply to "get saved." Don't view it as elementary school from which you move on to more mature Christian matters. We never graduate from the gospel. You and I, as believers, desperately need the preaching of the gospel. I don't mean that we need a steady stream of evangelistic sermons. What I mean is we need the unfolding of the gospel in everything, in all of life, in all the matters that make up life. We need to see how all the dimensions of life find their God-ordained direction, measure, and meaning from the gospel.

Why do I need to hear the gospel again and again, at ever deeper levels?

Perhaps the hymn writer said it best: "Prone to wander, Lord, I feel it, prone to leave the God I love."[1]

Paul asked the Galatian believers, "Having begun by the Spirit, are you now being perfected by the flesh?" (Gal. 3:3).

No! Both the beginning of the Christian life and the unfolding of it are by grace—gospel grace. We start by grace, and we are sanctified by grace. We set out in this new relationship with God by grace, and we will only continue in that relationship by grace.

Far too many people accept Jesus as their Savior, receive the gift, and then get on with trying to live the Christian life by their own grinding efforts to do better and be better. The euphoric and profound rest they found in Christ's finished work has given way to a life of exhausting and frustrating trying.

A person prays to receive Christ. It has been made clear to her that this is a free gift of God's grace. She understands it is not available on the basis of her efforts, works, or religion. She is thrilled and joyously receives Christ and His salvation. The euphoria lasts a few weeks, perhaps. But over time, as she gets involved in church and makes friends with many Christians, she begins to stockpile many new *oughts* and *shoulds*. Her heart wanders from the rest she found in Christ's finished work, and she begins to tell herself, "I ought" to be this and "I should" do that. So what does she do? The natural, human thing. She starts trying—*really hard*—to be and do what she thinks Jesus wants her to be and do.

But she can't.

She begins to live her Christian life in a kind of gospel disconnect. It leads to—do I dare say it?—a *Christian* despair. Discouragement moves into disappointment, which gives way to despair—and all in the name of Christ! Having begun her new life with the confession, *I can't, but God can*, she finds herself now cast down again with the realization, *I can't*. She has never come—*as a Christian*—to the blessed realization "I cannot—God never said I could; but *God can*, and always said He would!"[2]

God establishes our faith "according to" the gospel (Rom. 16:25). The gospel is the *standard* by which He establishes and keeps us. This is why Paul could say, "*as you received* Christ Jesus the Lord, *so walk* in him" (Col. 2:6). God saved you by grace; He will keep you by grace. The Christian life begins by grace; it continues by grace. We begin with God not on the basis of what we can do, but on what God has done and can do through Christ.

The gospel is also the *means* by which God establishes and keeps us. He firmly fixes us in faith through a constant return to the gospel and through interpreting all of life and relationship with God by the lenses of the gospel. If we view the gospel as something only to get us started, we will soon find the Christian life to be a disappointment. You will find yourself frustrated, exhausted, and even disillusioned.

The gospel is the ground in which we've been planted. Without it we wobble. And wobble is not good.

13

GOSPEL EVER!

Many people view *the gospel as the first step.* And let me affirm, you must take the first step! The first step is essential. No one begins the journey with God apart from the first step.

But having taken that first step, if you leave it behind and move on to maturity, leaving—in your mind's eye—the elementary gospel to graduate to higher truths, you err. This is a massive mistake, a colossal blunder.

Rather than the gospel as first step, let me suggest a different metaphor—*the gospel as North Star*. The North Star is there as you begin your journey. It is the means by which God guides you into relationship with Himself. But the North Star is always there, never really out of sight—the one fixed constant in the night's horizon. The one immovable, unchanging sign in a swirling, changing landscape of lights. By this North Star you not only begin your journey with God, but you continue on the journey with Him—ever checking in to take a reading on your experiences, your inclinations, your ideas, your tentative conclusions about things.

No matter where the journey may lead, no matter how hard the winds may blow or how high the waves may rise, no matter how dark the night may become, you can always find the North Star of the gospel and take a reading of your position and the direction you must move next.

God establishes us in faith by the gospel. But notice what the text says. God establishes us not simply by the gospel but by the gospel *preached.* God is able to establish you in faith, says the apostle, "according to my gospel and the preaching of Jesus Christ" (Rom. 16:25).

These are not two different things: "my gospel" and "the preaching of Jesus Christ." No, the second elaborates upon the first. The "preaching of Jesus Christ" expounds upon, enlarges upon, and makes more specific what Paul meant by "my gospel."

Note that the gospel is something that *must be proclaimed.* It can't just be read—in the Bible or in a book about the Bible. This in no way diminishes the Bible or any book that communicates the gospel. It simply recognizes what the Bible itself says—the gospel is something that must be *spoken.* It must be *heard.* The gospel, by its very nature, requires *proclamation.* And notice if you will what is at the center of that proclamation: a person—Jesus Christ!

There is here a double emphasis. There is and must be *personal* proclamation—one person telling another the gospel. This is evangelism. It must take place. Someone spoke the gospel to you. Who was it? How did it happen?

There must also be a *collective* proclamation. The Christians in Rome had already heard the gospel and believed. Someone proclaimed the gospel to them. Perhaps some of those present at Pentecost (Acts 2:10), when the Spirit was given and Peter preached so powerfully, returned and spoke the gospel to their family, friends, and acquaintances. Maybe they too believed. In one way or another someone told them the gospel, and they believed by God's grace. But Paul is now talking to them as a collective whole, as a body of Christians. His message is this: You still need to hear and sit under the on going proclamation of the gospel.

Why? Because all of life, not just its beginning, is by grace!

We need to sit under a steady stream of explanation about the grace God continues to extend to us in the gospel. We need to hear the gospel not just to "get saved," but to be saved every day—indeed, every moment of every day. The Bible speaks of salvation in three tenses: We *have been* saved (Eph. 2:8), we *are being* saved (2 Cor. 2:15), we *will be* saved (1 Cor. 3:15).

In every case it is the grace of God extended to you in the person of Jesus Christ that is the answer, the power, the effective means of God's saving work in your life.

May I ask, what do you need God to save you from today? From what addiction? From what relationship issues? From what folly? From what self-righteousness? From what delusional attempt at self-effort? From what besetting sin?

In all cases the answer is found in the free grace God desires to make real within you in the person of Jesus Christ.

We all need to regularly come together to hear the gospel proclaimed to us again and again, so we understand how God's grace is being extended to us today, saving us from all that besets us.

God keeps us by the gospel *preached*. But that is not all that Paul says. Look again. We are told that God establishes our faith by the gospel preached *from the Bible*.

God is able to establish you "according to the revelation of the mystery that was kept secret for long ages but has now been disclosed and through the prophetic writings [the Old Testament Scriptures] has been made known" (Rom. 16:25–26).

We need not merely someone's testimony about faith in Christ and how He has saved them, wonderful and appropriate as such testimonies are. We need more than someone's theological musings about Jesus and what He did. Such discoursing has a place. But what we really need is gospel grace unfolded for us *from the text of the Bible*.

Can you put your finger on it in your Bible? Can you look it up again later and see it in your Bible? When the testifier or the theologian are absent and all that remains is you, your troubles, temptations, and trials—and God and His Word—can you put your finger on the text from which gospel grace has been shown you? Are you able then to go to God in His Word and experience personally that grace in your hour of need?

This is what we truly need!

God has built Bible preaching into the fabric of how He intends to extend His grace into our lives. God intends that His people gather weekly for worship. Under the light of God's Word many things are to happen during that time—praise in song, prayer, giving, and the reading of Scripture are among them. But the centerpiece of our time together is to be the preaching of God's Word. The Bible is how we hear God's voice to us. The Bible is the means by which God intends to make clear to us how His grace looks today, this week in our lives.

So what's God's solution to our predisposition to wobble? Establishing us—fixed, immovable, solid, and steady in Christ. How has He determined to achieve that? *By the gospel . . . preached . . . from the Bible.*

14

GOSPEL PERSPECTIVE

Preaching is not something to which most folks are anxious to subject themselves. That's putting it mildly.

Several forces oppose it in our day. In a relativistic culture, people want to know why your version of truth is more valid than the one the other guy promotes. The pluralistic impulse of our age works against any notion of truth in any absolute sense. Even if one affirms the idea of absolute truth and even if one believes it to be found only in the revelation of Jesus Christ given us in the written Word of God, he's likely to wonder why hearing someone else expound it is essential.

So it's only fair to ask: *Why is preaching the gospel from the text of the Bible the effective means in establishing God's children?*

It is effective because it is in the gospel that God unites eternity past with eternity future, revealing the strategic position of the present time in view of both. It is in this that we are lifted to live beyond simply the immediate.

Where preaching is valued, or at least endured, there is a great cry for preaching that is relevant. But just what is *relevant* preaching? If you were to poll the people in any given church this Sunday, you would probably leave with as many definitions as worshipers. You'll find one is struggling with depression, so for that one a relevant sermon is one which speaks of depression. Another is wrestling with a major life-changing decision, so a relevant sermon is one about knowing

God's will. The people on either side of these two wrestle with their own issues. If relevant preaching is the ability to touch on the specific issue on a given person's heart at that present moment, then the preacher doesn't stand a chance.

May I suggest a different understanding of what makes for relevant preaching? Truly relevant preaching is that which connects the present with eternity past and with eternity future.

Clearly the apostle is pursuing such lofty matters, for he speaks here of "long ages" (lit., "in times eternal," Rom. 16:25), of "the eternal God" (v. 26), and of "forevermore" (v. 27).

In Paul's doxology of praise, we discover that the gospel *makes sense of what God has done in eternity past*. The gospel is "according to the revelation of the mystery that was kept secret for long ages but has now been disclosed and through the prophetic writings has been made known to all nations, according to the command of the eternal God" (vv. 25–26).

By "mystery" Paul does not mean something eerie and mysterious, but something which heretofore had not been disclosed. In eternity past God established a plan. He has been working that plan throughout history. He disclosed this plan to humanity in progressive steps of revelation. Each revelation was a gift, not something owed to us. Each was a grace. Step by step God has informed us of what He was up to. Each step further explained the previous steps. But there was a poignant moment in human history ("has now been disclosed") when light was given that illuminated and made sense of what had gone before and what yet lies ahead.

That moment was the entrance of Jesus Christ into the world and the completion of the saving mission given Him in His first advent. Climactic clarity has come in the revelation of the gospel of Jesus Christ. We look back now upon the Old Testament Scriptures and realize that, though at the time they did not completely understand what God was doing, we can see it now through the lenses of the gospel.

Some things become clearer as we view them in the rearview mirror. That view is ours through the gospel.

We long for our lives to connect to something bigger than we are, something eternal, to discover we are a part of something that lasts, that endures, that matters ultimately. That connection is made when we embrace the gospel in repentant faith and continue exploring its depths and dimensions in all of life.

The gospel not only makes sense of what God has been doing from eternity past, it also *makes sense of what God will yet do in eternity future*. The praise crescendoes: "to the only wise God be glory forevermore through Jesus Christ!" (v. 27).

Glory is God's goal. It has been from the inception of His plan. This has been His pursuit from the conception of the plan to the creation of all that is and will be to the closing of human history.

Is it permissible to ask, why is glory a worthy goal for God? It would not be worthy as an ultimate goal for you or me. So why is it appropriate for God?

It is because He alone is God (v. 27). He alone is "able" (v. 25). He alone is "eternal" (v. 26). He alone is "wise" (v. 27).

C. S. Lewis was correct: "The glory of God . . . is the real business of life."[1]

In 1963 a sign was hung on the door of a defunct church in New York: "Gone out of business. Didn't know what our business was."

Our business—along with planets, petunias, and peacocks (as well as all the rest of creation)—is the glory of God. God made it our business. If we don't know what it is and don't pursue its success, we labor in vain and waste our years.

The gospel makes sense of both the past and the future. For that reason it alone *makes sense of what God is doing at present*.

15

GOSPEL OBEDIENCE

Standing here between the eternity behind us and the yawning chasm of eternity before us, God's purpose for our lives is to bring "all nations" into "the obedience of faith" (Rom. 16:26). Check it out; you'll discover that this is what Paul has been about from the beginning of this long explanation of the gospel: "for the sake of his name among all the nations" (Rom. 1:5).

Ponder that: "the obedience of faith."

This is precisely how the New Testament described someone who came to salvation: "a great many [i.e., a large number] of the priests became *obedient to the faith*" (Acts 6:7). This is the standard by which God will judge in the end who are truly His people and who are not: "inflicting vengeance on those who do not know God and on those who do not obey the gospel of our Lord Jesus" (2 Thess. 1:8).

Clearly, we are not saved by obeying. Salvation is a gift, from first to last. A gift received by faith. But the gift is given to bring about obedience, which is enabled by that same grace of God. Post-conversion obedience is the testimony that the gift indeed has been received. Disobedience testifies that it has not truly been welcomed, whatever other claims we may make.

As Oswald Chambers has said, "The best measure of a spiritual life is not its ecstasies, but its obedience."[1]

God establishes us as His children through the gospel . . . preached . . . from the Bible. This means is effective because it gathers up eternity past and eternity future in the invitation to what God is doing in the present hour.

What is the great apostle's last word on this matter? What appropriate word closes this magnificent letter to the Romans? It is, simply, "Amen."

"Amen" is brought over to us from Hebrew via Greek and into our English translations. It means something like "let it be so" or "truly." It is employed as an affirmation of something just stated. Yet it comes from a verb meaning "firm" or "fixed." That sounds very much like "establish" (Rom. 16:25 NKJV), doesn't it?

God's purpose (to establish) has now become our confession and confidence (amen).

The amen of your obedience tamps the soil of truth around your life, fixing you firmly in Christ. As we hear the gospel again and again and again proclaimed through God's Word (not just to "get saved" but to continue "being saved" each moment of each day), and as we add our heart's amen to it, we are cooperating with what God has been seeking from all of eternity past, what He is working toward in eternity future, and what He is doing in the present hour.

Our most important amen is not a verbal one but a volitional one—the amen of trusting obedience.

The amen of your obedience lashes your present challenge backward into eternity past and forward into eternity future, fixing you steadfast and immovable in faith and obedience in the present.

PART FOUR

GOD IS ABLE TO RESCUE YOU

Because he himself has suffered when tempted, he is able to help those who are being tempted.

Hebrews 2:18

16

THE TRUTH ABOUT TEMPTATION

Temptation is a tyrant, an oppressor, a despot.

Temptation is a universal human struggle. It is no respecter of age, striking the AARP folks and preschoolers alike, the boomer and the millennial without distinction. Temptation cares not your gender.

Economics can't buy your way out of temptation. No tax bracket is exempt from temptation's tug.

Temptation barges its way into the households and lives of people across every strata of society. It makes itself at home in both the trailer park and the penthouse. There is no culture where temptation is not found, nor is there one where it is more dominant than another.

You can't educate temptation out of the human experience. It strikes the Harvard grad as well as the high school dropout. No amount of religious exercises can excise it from your life completely.

Temptation is common to the single and to the married, to the aged and the young, to the rich and the poor, to the important and to the unnoticed, to the powerful and to the weak, to the healthy and the infirm, to the educated and to the uneducated, to the religious and to the irreligious.

Temptation is the common experience of every person.

Temptation comes in many forms. It slaps you in the face in audacious boldness. Then it whispers in your ear with seductive secrecy.

At times it plants a thought; at others it presents an image. Sometimes we are aware of its arrival, and at times we are blinded to its approach.

Temptation is a universal human struggle.

Temptation is watching over your shoulder and whispering in your ear even as your eyes scan these lines.

We are tempted to judge others by what they wear, by how they act, by where they sit, by whom they talk to. We are tempted to think that our religious routine merits something before God. We are tempted to judge the music, the preacher, the praying, and the services of the church. We are tempted to desire another person's spouse. We are tempted to sell ourselves as better than we are in reality. We are tempted to lie when asked how we are doing.

On and on and on we could go, but you know what I'm talking about.

All pervasive as temptation is and as all powerful as it can appear, God is able to deliver you from its clutches. Jesus "is able to help those who are being tempted" (Heb. 2:18).

I want you know this, but I want you to do more than know it, for all good Bible-believing Christians believe this is possible with God. I want you to actively *believe* that God *will* deliver you in temptation.

Read that line of Scripture in its fuller context:

> Since therefore the children share in flesh and blood, he himself likewise partook of the same things, that through death he might destroy the one who has the power of death, that is, the devil, and deliver all those who through fear of death were subject to lifelong slavery. For surely it is not angels that he helps, but he helps the offspring of Abraham. Therefore he had to be made like his brothers in every respect, so that he might become a merciful and faithful high priest in the service of God, to make propitiation for the sins of the people. For because he himself has suffered when tempted, he is able to help those who are being tempted. (Heb. 2:14–18)

You and I both know the feeling that comes over us when temptation strikes. But what do you suppose is the response of heaven when temptation slithers up next to you?

17

THE MOMENT OF TEMPTATION

Temptation appears in a moment of time. Suddenly, unannounced, seemingly out of nowhere, it overtakes you. Is that why we assign the verb "strike" to the event? Temptation *strikes*—like a lightning bolt, like a rattlesnake, like a fist circling in from your blind side.

A lot transpires in that moment—much of it, of course, is negative. But the Bible tells us that at the moment temptation strikes, some wonderful things also transpire.

For example, the moment temptation strikes, *Jesus' heart goes out to you*. It was for this very reason that Jesus "had to be made like [us as] his brothers in every respect, so that he might become a merciful and faithful high priest in the service of God" (Heb. 2:17).

Jesus is "merciful" in that He is sympathetic and compassionate toward us. In fact, in the original Greek text, the emphasis is placed upon "merciful." The original word order is: "that a merciful, he might become, and faithful high priest."

Mercy is that feeling you get when you see harm befall another. It's that inward gut groan when you see misfortune strike another. It is the cringe at the sight of pain.

As I type these lines, the headlines are focused on multiple deaths from a horrific train accident in Europe, on multiplied injuries caused by a massive propane explosion in Florida, and on accounts of over one hundred children rescued from sex trafficking in a police sting operation.

As I read these lines, an ache settles inside me. A groan arises that isn't always audible, but which is palpable. There is a pain, caused not by injury done to me, but inflicted upon others like me.

Do you dare believe that something like this happens in heaven the moment temptation presents itself to you?

Or at the moment temptation strikes again in your life, do you more readily picture divine disgust, anger or maybe even wrath?

Temptation isolates. A good portion of its power lies in its ability to separate and divide. Temptation splits you off by yourself, leaving you lonely, afraid, powerless, and feeling unloved, unnoticed, and inconsequential.

My dear friend, psychologist Dr. Donald Lichi, puts it so well: Strongholds are established in secrecy and enforced through silence.[1]

Temptation's presence is heard behind the hiss of lines like: "God is angry with you!" "No one understands your pressures or knows your needs!" "You owe it to yourself!"

Lies!

Know this: The moment temptation strikes, *Jesus' heart goes out to you*. He cares. He knows. He loves. He moves toward you.

More than this, know that *Jesus' hand goes out to you*. "For surely it is not angels that he helps, but he helps the offspring of Abraham" (v. 16).

The word twice translated "helps" has the idea of taking hold of, seizing, and taking to one's self.[2] The idea is helping or assisting by drawing another to your side.[3]

It is the hand over the side of the boat to the drowning victim.

It is the hand of the rescue team member to a climber trapped on the face of a mountain.

It is the hand reaching to the one who has fallen on the ice.

The moment you are tempted, look up! There is a hand stretching out to you. It is a strong, firm, loving hand.

When I was twenty years old, I was part of a challenging obstacle course. It was a team competition. Victory was found *together*; no solo performances there. Toward the end of the course loomed a smooth, vertical wall eleven feet high. Every member of the team had to go up and over that wall before victory could be achieved. That included the strong ones and the weak ones, the skinny ones and the . . . other ones, the athletic ones and the decidedly unathletic members of the team. Everyone had to go up and over. All we had was each other.

We got everyone up and over fairly quickly, except for one. In the end, lying flat atop the platform, multiple people sitting on my legs to keep me from going over the side, I hung everything from just below my belly button to the end of my outstretched hand downward toward that lone team member. He took a run, made a leap, and laid hold of my outstretched arm, . . . and there he was . . . dangling between heaven and earth, the entire endeavor resting upon the strength of my right arm.

My arm has never been all that strong. It is not nearly as strong now as it was then. Truly, "Cursed is the man who trusts in man and makes flesh his strength" (Jer. 17:5)!

We need a stronger arm. We need the arm of omnipotence—the arm that extends all the resources of heaven to us in our need. When the people of God faced a foe so overwhelming all hope seemed lost, king Hezekiah declared, "With him is an arm of flesh, but with us is the LORD our God, to help us and to fight our battles" (2 Chron. 32:8).

In that moment of temptation, as you near the tipping point that stands between victory and defeat, will you dare believe that all power is reaching out to you?

Just how does Jesus reach out?

The point is that Jesus helps (reaches out to) us as humans, as opposed to the angelic order. He reached out to humanity and took to Himself a human nature. When the second person of the Trinity came to earth, He did not divest Himself of deity, but in addition to His divine nature, He took a perfect human nature. Jesus is rightly called the God-man, being 100 percent both.

Jesus reached down to us by taking to Himself a human nature and by living in a human body with that nature. Jesus reached to us through the entire rescue effort He effected in the act of taking on humanity. We will examine that more fully in a moment, but for now know deeply and absolutely that at the moment of temptation Jesus' heart goes out to you, His hand goes out to you, and . . . *Jesus' help goes out to you.* Jesus "himself has suffered when tempted, [and thus] he is able to help those who are being tempted" (Heb. 2:18).

The word "help" translates a different Greek word than was translated similarly in verse 16. It comes from a compound word made up of "a cry" and "to run."[4] It means to jump and run at the cry of another—literally means "to run to the cry of a child."[5]

It is what parents do those initial weeks after their firstborn comes home from the hospital. They leap at a squawk, run at a whimper, and bolt for the bassinet at the first sound of discomfort or displeasure.

Count on this: When temptation comes to visit and you cry out under its trial, Jesus is already on His way.

When temptation strikes, Jesus' heart and hand and help go out to you, not just to comfort, but to deliver.

18

HOW JESUS RESCUES US WHEN TEMPTED

No one is as uniquely qualified to race to your aid in temptation as Jesus. That's because *toward the tempted, He is merciful.* "Therefore he had to be made like his brothers in every respect, so that he might become a merciful and faithful high priest in the service of God, to make propitiation for the sins of the people. For because he himself has suffered when tempted, he is able to help those who are being tempted" (Heb. 2:17–18).

The notion of Jesus' mercy, compassion, and understanding toward the tempted is not a sensation created by our imaginations. To a person who has lost a spouse, I can only say, "I can't tell you that I know what you're going through, because—thankfully—I've never been there. But I imagine it must be heart-rending!"

The compassion and mercy of Jesus, however, comes from firsthand experience.

Because Jesus took to Himself a sinless human nature, lived in a human body, and subjected Himself to the normal course of human development, birth, growth, and life, He understands what you are facing.

Jesus was tempted from His earliest conscious thoughts. Throughout His life He was tempted to avoid the cross. He was tempted by the Devil in wilderness (Matt. 4:8–11). He was tempted when the evil one worked through Peter (16:22–23). He was tempted while praying in Gethsemane (26:39).

Someone reading these lines will object, "No! Jesus could not have been tempted. He was fully divine. And God isn't subject to temptation."

But that is incorrect. True, Jesus was not tempted in His divine nature, for indeed "God cannot be tempted with evil" (James 1:13). Yet Jesus was tempted as to His human nature. "In the days of his flesh, Jesus offered up prayers and supplications, with loud cries and tears, to him who was able to save him from death, and he was heard because of his reverence. Although he was a son, he learned obedience through what he suffered" (Heb. 5:7–8).

Someone else objects, "Jesus was God! Temptation could not possibly have been as difficult for Him as it is for me!"

Jesus understands what you are going through when temptation calls. In fact Jesus understands your temptation *better* than you do.

Remember, Jesus never gave in to temptation. He "has been tempted as we are, yet without sin" (4:15).

When we succumb to temptation, we defend ourselves with comments like "I just couldn't take it anymore. I couldn't resist. The temptation was too strong." Yet for this very reason we never really experience the full strength of temptation. We cut the struggle short by giving in to the temptation.

How much longer would it have lasted? In what other ways would sin have presented itself to me? What other wiles and tricks would it have thrown at me?

Jesus, on the other hand, never gave in to sin. Thus He regularly faced the full fury of sin's assault. Jesus alone understands temptation's power, the depth of its depravity, and the cunning of its trickery.

C. S. Lewis wisely noted, "No man knows how bad he is till he has tried very hard to be good. A silly idea is current that good people do not know what temptation means. This is an obvious lie. Only those who try to resist temptation know how strong it is. . . . Christ, because He was the only man who never yielded to temptation, is also the only man who knows to the full what temptation means."[1]

Jesus alone knows how the tempted feel, and what we face. In this, however, He is helpful only because *toward the Father, Jesus is faithful.* He is a "faithful high priest in the service of God" (Heb. 2:17).

To what is Jesus faithful? His faithfulness found expression "in the service of God" ("in things pertaining to God," NASB). God the Son was sent on mission by God the Father. The Father laid out for Him a prescribed duty, a set course, a particular objective. Christ's sympathy toward us is only worth anything because of His faithfulness in fulfilling the Father's mission. The Father had some things that would have to be taken care of if He would relate to us in a way that is saving, loving, and gracious.

Just what was this mission to which Jesus has proven faithful? It was the divine mission "to make propitiation for the sins of the people" (v. 17).

I'll grant you, "propitiation" is a big and not-so-commonly-used word. It means to satisfy, conciliate, make well disposed toward.[2] As a holy God, His wrath was stirred up by our sin. We tend to define sin by what it does to us. That's not untrue or unimportant, but neither is it the beginning of the matter or its most important point. The starting and most essential point is what our sin is before and to God.

God is compelled, by the nature of His own justice and holiness, to bring injustice and unholiness into judgment. God can do nothing else but pour out His wrath against that which violates His nature, destroys His creatures, and seeks to derail His purposes. He could not possibly be a loving God and let such threats stand against His creatures. He could not possibly remain holy and wink at such affronts to His nature.

For that reason Jesus made propitiation for our sins. That is to say, Jesus satisfied the wrath of God against us. Through Jesus, God lovingly saves us from His own wrath! At the cross your sin was laid upon Jesus and credited to Him (Isa. 53:6). The judgment that was due to us for those sins was poured out by the Father upon His own Son, who He had made to stand in our place. All the infinite wrath of God's violated holiness fell upon Christ that it might never come back upon us. Jesus died our death. What would have taken us an eternity to bear—because it was an eternal debt against an eternal God—Jesus bore in that singular act. He could do so because He alone, being an eternal being, could pay that eternal price.

The result is that the wrath of God is satisfied. Your sin has already been judged. There is no more wrath in God toward you! Through His horrifying, agonizing separation from His Father, Jesus has reconciled you to His Father.

Jesus is perfectly and uniquely positioned to rescue you when temptation strikes. He is heartily, powerfully, effectually merciful toward you precisely because He has been fully faithful to His Father.

19

HOW JESUS RESCUES US WHEN TEMPTED (CONTINUED)

Toward the Father, Jesus was faithful, so that toward the tempted, He might be merciful. Both of these position Him so that *toward the Devil, He is successful.*

"Since therefore the children share in flesh and blood, he himself likewise partook of the same things, that through death he might destroy the one who has the power of death, that is, the devil, and deliver all those who through fear of death were subject to lifelong slavery" (Heb. 2:14–15).

After He created the first man, God told Adam: "You may surely eat of every tree of the garden, but of the tree of the knowledge of good and evil you shall not eat, for in the day that you eat of it you shall surely die" (Gen. 2:16–17). Indeed, "the wages of sin is death" (Rom. 6:23).

In this, Satan found a toehold. He has tempted us, and we've fallen. We have sinned, and we are justly vulnerable to him as the accuser (Rev. 12:10). We all feel intuitively the wages that must be paid out for our self-rule and independence. Death awaits us all.

It is in this sense that Satan had the power of death in his hand.

God controls death. "No man has power to retain the spirit, or power over the day of death" (Eccl. 8:8). "In his hand is the life of every living thing and the breath of all mankind" (Job 12:10). In God's "book were written, . . . the days that were formed for me, when as yet there was none of them" (Ps. 139:16).

If Satan can tempt a person to sin, he will cause the result of sin—which is death—to come upon him.

Follow the logic!

- *Death is the ultimate destination Satan desires for us*. Physically, death means the separation of spirit from body. Spiritually, death means the separation of your life from the life of God. Eternally, death means this state being sealed as your experience forever in hell. *Death* is the ultimate destination Satan desires for us, precisely because *life* is the destination God has intended for us.
- *Sin is the pathway to death*. "The wages of sin is death" (Rom. 6:23).
- *Temptation is the doorway to sin*. "But each person is tempted when he is lured and enticed by his own desire. Then desire when it has conceived gives birth to sin, and sin when it is fully grown brings forth death" (James 1:14–15).
- *So Jesus endured temptation Himself and then paid for our sins, thus breaking the power of the evil one and delivering us from the sentence of death*. Jesus took away the fear of death by taking the punishment for our sin and in so doing robbed Satan of his power to rob God of the glory due Him. "Since therefore the children share in flesh and blood, he himself likewise partook of the same things, that through death he might destroy the one who has the power of death, that is, the devil, and deliver all those who through fear of death were subject to lifelong slavery" (Heb. 2:14–15).

The destination (death) is no longer required because the pathway (sin) has been made unnecessary so that the doorway (temptation) is no longer irresistible.

You are able to give in to temptation, but you don't have to. You are able to sin, but you don't have to. You are able to continue down the path of sin and be separated from God in this life and forever in the next through death, *but you don't have to*!

That's what the Devil doesn't want you to know.

Jesus completely destroyed the Devil, his demons, and his kingdom plans when He died on the cross, rose again, and ascended to the right hand of the Father. "The reason the Son of God appeared was to destroy the works of the devil" (1 John 3:8). And He did His work exceedingly well. "He disarmed the rulers and authorities and put them to open shame, by triumphing over them in him" (Col. 2:15).

"Great!" you say. "But how do I recognize Jesus' hand and heart and help when they come to me?"

20

THE (FULL) TRUTH ABOUT TEMPTATION

To spot Jesus' hand, heart, and help reaching out to you in temptation, you'll need a new set of lenses—trifocals in this case.

First, when you are tempted, Jesus provides you *truth*, because in all temptation there's a *lie* going on.

The power of a temptation is in its falsehood. Every temptation is leveraged on a lie. Every time. Always. Without exception. Temptation is a sales pitch begging you to buy into a misperception of reality.

Jesus taught us that the Devil "does not stand in the truth, because there is no truth in him" and that "when he lies, he speaks out of his own character, for he is a liar and the father of lies" (John 8:44).

The antidote for falsehood is truth. A lie is undone by light. That is why Jesus said, "If you abide in my word, you are truly my disciples, and you will know the truth, and *the truth will set you free*" (John 8:31–32).

The Devil's arsenal of lies is vast, and we couldn't even begin to name them all here. He knows your vulnerabilities and forges falsehoods just to be aimed at you. But know this: The power of Satan's deception is in the lie. Expose the lie to truth, and it is rolled back just as darkness flees the sun each morning.

So here is how you'll recognize Jesus' hand reaching to you, His heart going out to you, His help coming to you—*Scripture will come to your mind*. Jesus promised the apostles He would send His Holy Spirit, saying He will "bring to your remembrance all that I have said to you"

(John 14:26). And after "he was raised from the dead, his disciples remembered [what Jesus] had said . . . and they believed the Scripture and the word that Jesus had spoken" (John 2:22). The Holy Spirit wants similarly to bring to our minds the Scriptures those apostles wrote down so we can act upon them in faith.

But the Holy Spirit isn't going to bring to your mind what you never put there. You must take in the Word before He will bring it back. We must be in the Bible, and the Bible must be in us. The Bible is not an anthology of inspirational stories, poems, and reflections meant simply to warm your heart or calm your nerves. It is the living Word of the living God. It is active and moving and working wherever it is spoken, read, and believed. It goes where nothing else in human experience can go. It is powerful beyond all human ability. It can do what your best intentions, attempts, and inclinations cannot. The Bible is God's mind revealed to us.

You gamers out there. Think of it like this—the Bible gives you the "cheat codes" to the all-too-real game of life!

When temptation strikes, Jesus sends you light via the Scriptures to expose the lie inherent in temptation. But that's only the beginning. When you are tempted, Jesus provides you *strength*, because in all temptation there's a *struggle* going on.

The Holy Spirit not only reminds us of what Jesus said, but mediates the very life of Jesus to us. The Holy Spirit is "the Spirit of Jesus" (Acts 16:7). With "the help of the Spirit of Jesus Christ" (Phil. 1:19) even the most difficult trial, darkest night, and despairing circumstances are transformed.

You had better find something in your battle with temptation that is stronger than your willpower. And, thank the Lord, that something is not a *thing* at all, but a person—the very indwelling presence of Christ through the ministry of His Spirit. As a believer, Jesus' own presence, life, and power reside in you by the power of the Holy Spirit.

When He spoke of the spiritual battle in which we find ourselves, the apostle Paul called us to "take . . . the sword of the Spirit, which is the word of God" while we are "praying at all times in the Spirit, with all prayer and supplication" (Eph. 6:17–18).

You'll recognize the hand and heart and help of Jesus approaching you, because you'll find yourself resisting temptation, even after your strength has run out. You will realize that you are hanging in there when you couldn't possible have done it on your own.

Ever seen the guy at the gym who is trying to bench press three hundred pounds? He's got the bar about three quarters of the way up, but has hit his limit. He can't push it any further. The bar has come to a momentary stop as he continues to push with all his might. It hasn't started a downward descent yet, but neither is it ascending. This guy's strength is finished; he simply hasn't admitted it yet. Then his friend—the spotter—takes a couple of fingers (just a couple of fingers on one hand) and applies just the slightest upward pressure. And *voila*! Up goes the bar! The man on the bench couldn't lift three hundred pounds. But he could lift two hundred ninety eight pounds. But it wasn't a two hundred ninety eight pound test, was it? The strength he needed had to come from beyond him.

There are some temptations that are only overcome by endurance. When you find yourself holding out, you realize you're being held up by a hand stronger than your own.

You'll recognize the hand, heart, and help of Jesus coming your way when truth comes to mind and when strength rises up. And when you are tempted, Jesus provides *escape*, because in all temptation there's a *trap* being set.

One famous tract begins with the axiom, "God loves you and has a wonderful plan for your life."[1] It is equally true—though not nearly so attractive—that Satan hates you and has a hideous plot for your eternal demise. There are such things as "the schemes of the devil" (Eph. 6:11), and they are aimed at followers of Jesus.

Some temptations are defeated only by endurance, but there are others you overcome only by escape. "No temptation has overtaken you that is not common to man. God is faithful, and he will not let you be tempted beyond your ability, but with the temptation he will also provide the way of escape, that you may be able to endure it" (1 Cor. 10:13).

Joseph fled Potiphar's wife (Gen. 39:12). So too we must "flee youthful passions and pursue righteousness, faith, love, and peace, along with those who call on the Lord from a pure heart" (2 Tim. 2:22).

You'll recognize Jesus drawing near as you see some route of relief and take it at all cost. Taking that escape might cost you your job, your friends, your reputation, your recreation, your computer—but a path there will be!

God's promise is this, when you are tempted you'll recognize the hand and heart and help of Jesus reaching out to you. He will see to it that His Word comes to your mind, that His strength will rise up within you, and that His appointed escape will open before you.

Oswald Chambers was right: "When it is a question of God's Almighty Spirit, never say 'I can't'. Never let the limitation of natural ability come in. If we have received the Holy Spirit, God expects the work of the Holy Spirit to be manifested in us."[2]

PART FIVE

GOD IS ABLE TO KEEP HIS PROMISES TO YOU

[Abraham was] fully convinced that God was able to do what he had promised.

Romans 4:21

21

A PROMISE-LED LIFE

"Helen Rennard wanted to be left alone. For most of her life, she succeeded. Then everything spiraled out of control."[1]

At eighty years of age Helen was ordered to vacate her crumbling, dilapidated home in Akron, Ohio. Housing authorities declared it a health hazard and public nuisance. Officials entered the home and found rooms piled high with moldering garbage, remains of unusable furniture, cast off containers, and clothing. Buckets caught reeking water descending through a leaky ceiling. Rodents feasted on fetid garbage piled high in the basement. Helen had long ago boarded up the doors, so she climbed in and out of her home through a broken window. Helen lived in squalor and poverty.

In 1931 her husband abandoned her and their three children (the last of which she was still pregnant with at the time of his departure). She did the best she could to hold life and home together by cleaning houses, but unable to provide for her three children during the Great Depression, she sent them off to an orphanage in Columbus.

After that she just tried to hang on. Odd thing is, when city workers entered the home to begin preparing it for demolition, they discovered among the piles of rotting garbage "piles of out-of-circulation currency and collectible silver coins" hidden among the debris.[2] They unearthed over $85,000, the equivalent to $240,400 in today's economy. They also discovered bank documents which registered over $24,000 on deposit at local banks.[3]

When questioned, Helen replied simply, "I started hiding my money. . . . I guess I forgot where it was."[4]

Helen lived in squalor and isolated poverty, though she had more than enough financial means to have provided herself a decent home and a reasonable lifestyle.

Stories like this boggle the imagination. *Why live in poverty when you have the means to live in plenty?*

That is a question not only for Helen but also for you and me. Too many followers of Christ live below their wealth. And I'm not speaking in monetary terms.

The Bible tells us that God "has blessed us in Christ with every spiritual blessing in the heavenly places" (Eph. 1:3). The storehouses of heaven have an account with your name on it. The most recent statement reveals that "every spiritual blessing in the heavenly places" has been deposited to your account.

Yet we live too often like spiritual paupers, eking out an existence, just trying to hold out till Jesus comes.

That heavenly bank statement declares that "his divine power has granted to us all things that pertain to life and godliness"! Indeed, this is ours "through the knowledge of him who called us to his own glory and excellence, by which he has granted to us his precious and very great promises, so that through them you may become partakers of the divine nature, having escaped from the corruption that is in the world because of sinful desire" (2 Peter 1:3–4).

These promises are made to us by one who cannot lie, who is always faithful to His word, and who has extended these promises to us with our good in mind. We do God no favor when we live below the level of His promises. There is no virtue in living below the promise line of God's grace.

Those counted among the godly throughout the ages have been those who believed God for His promises and acted upon them in faith, believing that God is both able and willing to keep the promises He makes to His people.

Consider as our example Abraham—the father of our faith. His story is first recounted in Genesis 12–25. Later writers of Scripture reflect upon and draw implications from his walk with God (Rom. 4; Gal. 3; Heb. 6, 7, 11). Consider with me Abraham, drawing upon all of these passages, but largely focusing upon the apostle Paul's words in the fourth chapter of Romans.

God promised Abraham, "I have made you the father of many nations" (Rom. 4:17). God invited him to look at the stars and then promised him, "So shall your offspring be" (v. 18). Vast, immense, magnificent promises!

Yet, "his own body . . . was as good as dead (since he was about a hundred years old)" and then there was the matter of "the barrenness of Sarah's womb" (v. 19). "No unbelief made him waver concerning the promise of God, but he grew strong in his faith as he gave glory to God, fully convinced that God was able to do what he had promised" (vv. 20–21).

We are called to be "imitators of those who through faith and patience inherit the promises" (Heb. 6:12). Abraham is their headliner. Like him, the others "through faith . . . obtained promises" (11:33).

If you are like me, you want to know: How does that work? What does such faith look like? How do I live a promise-led life? How do I draw upon my grace-laden account in heaven?

In an attempt to answer those questions, I invite you to consider the anatomy of a promise kept. As I look at Abraham's life of faith (as described in Romans 4), I see several elements in the anatomy of a promise kept, each building and resting upon the others.

All through this process, I've been fighting the memory of a song. I'm just going to stop fighting and let it rip. I don't know if you've ever heard it before, but here is how it goes:

> Faith, mighty faith
> The promise sees
> And looks to God alone
> Laughs at impossibilities
> And cries, "It shall be done!"
> And cries, and cries, "It shall be done!"
> And cries, and cries, "It shall be done!"
> Laughs at impossibilities
> And cries, "It shall be done!"[5]

I hope it gets stuck in your heart as it has in mine, for we'll come back to it along our way.

22

STARTING STRAIGHT: GOD AND GRACE

It's no surprise that a promise-led life begins with God. Immediately the spotlight is on Him: "God was able to do what he had promised" (Rom. 4:21). God's ability is unimpeded, for the tense of "was able" underscores the ongoing, unending nature of His capacity. "Jesus Christ is the same yesterday and today and forever" (Heb. 13:8). "I the Lord do not change" (Mal. 3:6). What God was able to do in Abraham's day, He is able to do today. God stands ready at this moment to keep all His promises to you, just as He has in the lives of all the spiritual giants throughout history.

While it is true that God is continuously able to keep all His promises to you, it is also true that such fulfillment is realized in a moment in time. The aorist tense of the Greek verb translated "to do" points to something that happens at a particular moment in time. The God who never changes, remaining always the same from Abraham's day to ours (indeed, from all of eternity!), is able to show up in specific moments and in specific places of your life, bringing the fulfillment of His promises to your life. What God could do in Abraham's day, He can do in this day. What He did for Abraham, He can do for you.

A. W. Tozer was spot-on: "Anything God has ever done at any time, He can do now. And, anything God has ever done anywhere, He can do here. Furthermore, anything God has ever done in and through anyone, He is prepared to do through you."[1]

Everything begins with God. So we had better get to know Him. Or put another way, the character of God is foundational to a promise-led life.

It is imperative that we become students of God's character. We discover God's character from the Bible and internalize it through prayer. But we must also determine that we will—by His mercy and grace—know Him in our *experience*.

So with Bible in hand and knees firmly planted on the ground, you will discover that God is, among other things, faithful. The fulfillment of any promise rests upon God's faithfulness. "Let us hold fast the confession of our hope without wavering, for he who promised is faithful" (Heb. 10:23).

Let's be clear at this point. When drawing on your heavenly account, your faith rests upon God, not the promise. This might seem like an unnecessarily hairsplitting distinction, but that is what the Bible seems to tell us. God stated the promise to Abraham: "I have made you the father of many nations" (Rom. 4:17). Then Paul pointed immediately to the object of Abraham's trust for the fulfillment of that promise: "the God in whom he believed" (v. 17). It wasn't so much that Abraham believed in the promise, but that he believed in the God who issued and stood behind that promise.

Not long ago there was a company in our area which specialized in window replacement. They advertised heavily. Many people bought in. One great selling point was the lifetime guarantee that stood behind the windows. Sadly, many seized on the sales point only later to discover the company had gone out of business. There was no one to answer the phone. There was no phone to answer! No customer satisfaction department existed. Nothing. Gone.

A promise is only as good as the one making it. That is why the Bible tells us everything begins with God—the eternal, always faithful, unchanging one. He is the heart of a promise-led life.

Now as you look upon God through His Word, you discover that He deals with us in grace. Grace is the second element we must consider.

God dealt with Abraham in such a way "that the promise may rest on grace" (v. 16). Every promise rests upon God and upon that in His character which moves Him to extend His goodness and promises—grace.

Not everyone sees this about God. Sometimes pain and perplexities blind us to the evidences of God's grace.

Consider Job, the ancient sufferer. He knew nothing of the heavenly wager between the Evil One and God. He had no idea why he suffered. Under unrelenting pain his thoughts began to swirl, and he charged God with injustice. The book that bears his name recounts round after round of the counsel of Job's friends and Job's response to each. Eventually, when the counselors' counsel had played out, God cleared His throat and broke the silence. In the face of Job's questioning, God addressed him with scores of his own questions (Job 38–41). At the heart of all these God asks, "Who has first given to me, that I should repay him? Whatever is under the whole heaven is mine" (41:11).

Job could not possibly have understood the ultimate reason for his suffering. Under the weight of such mystery and pain, he questioned God. You and I would as well.

God's answer was to ask, "Who beat me to the punch in grace? Who has first given to me? To whom am I beholden? To whom do I owe anything?" Translation—"Job, I know that you hurt. I know that you don't understand why these things have befallen you. But listen, I don't owe you an explanation, let alone anything else. You are in no position to call me to account or demand anything of me."

Paul, the great apostle, wrestled with the mystery of God's dealings with his kinsmen, the Jews. He didn't understand entirely just why Jewish hearts were so hardened toward Jesus, the Christ. He didn't entirely understand how God could use them and then set them aside as a nation and welcome the Gentiles into His salvation. He wrestled to make theological sense of these mysteries in Romans 9–11. In the end he succumbed to the mystery of it all and ended where every theologian must eventually arrive—at the place of worship: "Oh, the depth of the riches and wisdom and knowledge of God! How unsearchable are his judgments and how inscrutable his ways!" (Rom. 11:33). And then he quoted God from His encounter with Job: "Or who has given a gift to him that he might be repaid?" (v. 35).

As God had reminded Job, so now Paul affirms to his readers—God owes us nothing! There is much we do not understand. We scratch our heads. Inquiring minds want to know. We can, and should, ask. Bring your questions to God. Just don't begin questioning God. Everything—*everything!*—is by grace. For each matter you do not understand, look at something God has given you to understand. For every mystery you must live with, find a promise that you must live by. Be honest with your questions; be relentless in seeing the grace God has extended to you.

Listen, there is no entitlement. You don't deserve any of the good things you enjoy. They are not yours by right. God owes us nothing!

Yet He does give. He is gracious.

We have no legal case against God, yet His promises are *guaranteed.* Indeed, the promise to Abraham was "guaranteed to all his offspring" (Rom. 4:16).

When you find a divine promise in the Bible, consider it as a certificate of redemption to be presented at the throne of God.

When I go with friends to a professional baseball game, we always stop by the designated driver booth before we find our seats. We fill out the form and receive in return a slip of paper that can be taken to one of the ballpark's concession stands to be redeemed for a glass of Coke.

All I have to do is present the paper, and they hand me an ice-cold glass of Coke. It is mine, gratis. What a deal!

When you put your finger upon a promise of God in your Bible, turn in prayer to God and present your certificate of redemption. The surety of the guarantee rests upon the character of God. What He has promised He will provide, for He is gracious by nature.

23

STAYING STRAIGHT: PROMISE

It is God's grace that moves Him to extend His promises.

You've been fairly silent to this point, but I know you're busting to ask it. So go ahead.

OK, what is the promise? What are God's promises?

I'm glad you asked! Thank you.

There are two sides of the promise coin, which we must consider: There is the promise of the gospel, and there are gospel promises. There is entering into eternal life, and there is living eternal life. You must receive the first (based upon the promise of the gospel) in order to be eligible for the second.

What is the promise of the gospel?

Listen carefully.

Jesus *lived* to provide the righteousness you lack (for righteousness is our fundamental need before a holy God). He *died* to pay the penalty you incurred for your independence from Him (for that is our fundamental failure before a holy God). He *lives again* to produce in and through you what God requires of you (for this is the promise of our holy God).

Sins forgiven. Righteousness extended. Life, indwelling and transforming you. This is the promise of the gospel.

Paul stated the promise this way, "If you confess with your mouth that Jesus is Lord and believe in your heart that God raised him from the dead, you will be saved" (Rom. 10:9).

If you have received, through repentance and faith in Jesus Christ, the promised gift of forgiveness, righteousness, and life, you are now in a position to begin to live a promise-led life. He has brought you within reach of all the gospel promises!

When it comes to identifying a God-given promise, remember two things. First, *be clear to whom the promise was given.* Not everything in the Scripture is a promise to you as a New Testament child of God. This is true especially as you read the Old Testament. Some of the promises you'll find there were specifically given to the nation of Israel. But there are other promises which are extended to us along with those who at that time were the people of God.

Second, *be certain about the time of the guaranteed fulfillment of each promise.* God has committed to the total fulfillment of some promises only at the return of Christ to earth. As you identify a promise, you must look for an indication of the time for the promise to be fulfilled. "But as *the time of the promise drew near*, which God had granted to Abraham, the people increased and multiplied in Egypt" (Acts 7:17). It was "thus [that] Abraham, *having patiently waited*, obtained the promise" (Heb. 6:15).

You can count on it—patience will be woven into the fabric of a promise-led life.

God's promises are given to promote God's purpose. In individual terms, that is ultimately your conformity to the character of Christ (Rom. 8:29). And character is often forged in the waiting room rather than the delivery room.

How long must I wait?

Good question. I wish I knew.

It may be longer than this life. "These all died in faith, not having received the things promised, but having seen them and greeted them from afar, and having acknowledged that they were strangers and exiles on the earth" (Heb. 11:13).

And don't let that sound like bad news, because it's not.

Just the other day, as I was wrestling in prayer before God over a difficult assignment and what appears to be my waning strength, the thought bolted through my mind, "I don't have to do this forever, just for the rest of my life."

I grinned. Right there in the middle of prayer. Honestly, I did. I chuckled right out loud as a smile played out across my face.

Strange, I know, but it somehow seemed a great relief to me. For, after all, we are built to outlive this life.

Take, for example, the matter of physical healing. Psalm 103 boldly describes God as the one "who heals *all* your diseases" (v. 3).

Really! I mean, honestly, "*all* your diseases"?

Jesus died to pay for all sin and all sin's effects. There is no other atonement, no other answer for sin or any part of sin's disastrous effects. And that includes the effects of sin upon our mortal bodies. The promise of a whole, perfect body was paid for at the cross of Jesus Christ.

Sadly, however, some have wrongly deduced from this that physical healing is always God's will in this present life and that if you don't experience it, the problem lies with you. "Weak faith, sin unconfessed, something," one will tell you with a thunderous tremor in the voice, "stands between you and the fulfillment of God's promise!"

Too many have been scarred by such nonsense. It qualifies as pastoral malpractice in my book.

Just read the Book! Yes, sometimes God does extend His mighty hand and heal physical bodies. You can't read the Bible without it being pushed right up in your face again and again. But neither can you honestly read the Bible and fail to notice that He does not always do so.

Why? What's the difference? Why for one and not for another?

Mystery!

The answer which we are to rest in throughout our sojourn through this world is that the promise's guarantee isn't for this life, but for the time of Christ's coming. For then our bodies will enter into the fullness of redemption from sin's curse, a redemption whose price was fully paid at the cross, but whose *guaranteed* fulfillment isn't yet in this life. Yes, we can and should seek God for healing (James 5:13–18). But we must rest in His wise determination as to whether He graciously extends such to us now, or has other, higher purposes for allowing us to walk the road of physical trouble and weakness (2 Cor. 12:1–10).

Everything begins with God, who, we discover, deals in grace. Such grace is extended to us in the form of His promises. Those promises then awaken within us something . . . oh, what shall we call it? It is something decidedly sweet, bright, luminous. Perhaps we can call it . . . hope!

24

STAYING STRAIGHT: HOPE AND FAITH

When you encounter God and discern that His intent toward you is entirely gracious and that His commitment to grace is voiced through specific promises made to you and recorded in the Bible, hope begins to rise up within you.

Suddenly it comes clear: *This is not all up to me!* There is one stronger, wiser, bigger than I am. He is intent not on my destruction, but on giving, gracing, loving, and blessing me. That grace and love is articulated and made specific and put into written form via specific promises.

Who writes a contract, binding themselves legally to costly action, when they don't have to?

Only God!

Notice that hope precedes faith. Of Abraham it was said, "In hope he believed" (Rom. 4:18).

Little wonder Peter spoke of the promises as "precious and very great," for through them the assurance is nothing less than being able to "become partakers of the divine nature" (2 Peter 1:4).

The promise is not just that God will do things for us, or on our behalf, but that He intends to share His very self and life with us.

Hope springs forth in faith.

God's promise must be met by my faith. Faith is expressed in prayer and proven in obedience.

Often you will find God has laid a condition alongside His promise. The promise is not fulfilled by our doing whatever is prescribed. But the promise is fulfilled in the context of relationship to God. The condition is almost always laid out as a pathway to deeper relationship to God.

"By faith Abraham obeyed when he was called to go out to a place that he was to receive as an inheritance. And he went out, not knowing where he was going. By faith he went to live in the land of promise" (Heb. 11:8–9).

Nothing is able to keep God from keeping His promises in your life. It is He who "gives life to the dead and calls into existence the things that do not exist" (Rom. 4:17).

Nothing. Not death. Not "impossible" circumstances. Nothing can stop God from keeping His promises in and to and through you.

Faith is not a vague feeling. It always rests upon a specific word from God. "In hope he believed . . . *as he had been told*" (v. 18). Abraham had a specific promise to lean upon. It wasn't a deduction drawn from God's general demeanor toward him. God had spoken specifically to him with a precise promise.

Our promises are found in the Bible. God is specific in making them. They are captured in words. They are found on a page. You can put your finger on them, underline them, memorize them, and post them on handwritten notes in places you'll be likely to see them often.

Miles Stanford was correct when he said, "True faith must be based solely on scriptural *facts*, for 'faith cometh by hearing, and hearing by the word of God' (Rom. 10:17). Unless our faith is established on facts, it is no more than conjecture, superstition, speculation, or presumption."[1]

Always be certain you can *put your finger on the promise*!

George Mueller was right, "Impressions have neither one thing nor the other to do with faith. Faith has to do with the Word of God. It is not impressions, strong or weak, which will make the difference. We have to do with the Written Word and not ourselves or our impressions."[2]

Faith is not based on impressions or probabilities but upon certainties! Alexander Hay said, "There must be definite knowledge of God's purpose and will" as we cast ourselves upon God's promise.[3]

Even in this be careful. Remember, faith rests not so much on the promise as on the one who issued it.

Faith is only as good as its object; a promise only as good as the one who made it.

Therefore, my trust is only as great as my knowledge of that object.

For this reason, the practice of praise and worship cultivates faith. Faith, to change the metaphor, is built on what God has revealed of Himself in the Bible (Rom. 10:17). Worship sets our eyes and rests our hearts upon the character of Him who is able. Abraham, "grew strong in his faith as *he gave glory to God*" (Rom. 4:20).

> "Faith, mighty faith
> The promises sees
> And looks to God alone."[4]

25

ARRIVAL: FULFILLMENT

If the promise is strength, you receive strength. If the promise is wisdom, you receive wisdom. If the promise is forgiveness, you receive forgiveness. If the promise is comfort, it is comfort you receive. If the promise is deliverance in temptation, a way will open up for you.

Do you want to live in the fulfillment of God's promises?

Here's what you do.

Find a specific promise of God in the Bible. That might take some work and time on your part, but it will be worth the effort.

Put your finger on the promise. I'm serious. Literally, do it. You cannot simply go by hunches, impressions, or deductions of what you'd like God to say or what you think maybe He said. Find an inscribed, inscripturated promise of God in black-and-white in your Bible.

Now, pray. First, *praise God*. Worship Him. Give Him glory. You're not buttering up God to convince Him to be good to you. You're declaring to heaven and earth the great worth of God. Now, *thank God* for His grace. Recount the ways He's already demonstrated His grace to you. Then, *tell God of your need*. Be honest. Don't worry about emotions one way or the other—if they show up or if they don't. Just use plain language to tell God what you need. Do it as authentically as you are able. Then, with your finger on the text of Scripture, say, "God I find in your Word that you have promised me as your child . . ." At this point quote, the promise of God. *Ask God to honor His Word* and name by keeping this promise in your life. The psalmist said, "You have exalted above all things your name and your word" (Ps. 138:2). Know that it is God's delight to honor His name by keeping His Word. Thus, by faith, *thank Him for how He will do so* in your life.

> My brother, if you have a divine promise, you need not plead it with an "if" in it; you may plead with a certainty. If for the mercy which you are now asking, you have God's solemnly pledged word, there will scarce be any room for the caution about submission to his will. You know his will: that will is in the promise; plead it. Do not give him rest until he fulfil it. He meant to fulfil it, or else he would not have given it. God does not give his words merely to quiet our noise, and to keep us hopeful for awhile, with the intention of putting us off at last; but when he speaks, he speaks because he means to act.[1]

Now wait on God. And in the process, keep your eyes open. The fulfillment of the promise may or may not come instantly, but it will come. It may not come in the form or manner you expected, but it will come.

All the while, keep your finger on that promise (write it out on a card; keep it with you; memorize it) and keep praying.

Finger on the promise and keep praying!

It is just as true today as it was in the first century: "You have need of endurance, so that when you have done the will of God you may receive what is promised" (Heb. 10:36).

I feel compelled to add this disclaimer, lest anyone get the wrong idea: The promises of God are not the assurance of a pain-free life of ease.

Many years ago, I led a worship service in which I centered on Hebrews 10:36. Here it is again, "You have need of endurance, so that when you have done the will of God you may receive what is promised." I led everyone in memorizing those words together, then we explored together their meaning. Among the worshipers was a dear brother in the Lord named Mike. I remember that Mike seemed especially moved by the words of this Scripture. He exhibited obvious, outward connection with them from the pew throughout the service. He approached me after the final amen and interacted with me about them before heading home.

Over the years Mike has proved the promise of those verses. First there came a horrible burn accident. Unspeakable pain. Long, lonely hours in a hospital burn unit. Questions! Surgery upon surgery. Then down along a rugged road, emergence back into the flow of life.

Then came the malaria. It entered his bloodstream while in Africa serving on a mission team sent from our church. It didn't show up until months later, well into normal life again at home. The doctors would hear no pleas from me or the other mission team members about its cause. Then came the call, "Pastor, come! Mike is slipping away." We prayed. Much. And God graciously answered, plucking Mike from the precipice of physical death. There lay before him another long, wearying road. But Mike was back. In fact he insisted on being a part of our next mission team to Africa.

Then came the call this past week, Mike fell twenty feet while repairing the roof on his house. Fractured skull. Broken ribs. Total life support.

As I write these lines we don't yet know the outcome of this most recent opportunity to believe the God of all grace for His promises. Yet we cling again to God, finger on the promise, the other hand raised to heaven: *Lord, please!*

Yes, there is much mystery in this life. But know this: "If you are Christ's, then you are Abraham's offspring, *heirs according to promise*" (Gal. 3:29).

> Faith, mighty faith
> The promise sees
> And looks to God alone
> Laughs at impossibilities
> And cries, "It shall be done!"
> And cries, and cries, "It shall be done!"
> And cries, and cries, "It shall be done!"
> Laughs at impossibilities
> And cries, "It shall be done!"[2]

PART SIX

GOD IS ABLE TO SUPPLY YOUR NEEDS

God is able to make all grace abound to you, so that having all sufficiency in all things at all times, you may abound in every good work.

2 Corinthians 9:8

26

I HAVE, THEREFORE I CAN

Congratulations! You've just won a million dollars.

Now, what are you going to do with the money?

We've all played that game, haven't we? Sometimes we are full of noble ideas—"I'd give half of the money to an orphanage in Haiti!" Other times we're more honest—"I would take a cruise and bypass Haiti!"

The question is built on the premise that there are things you could do if you had something you do not now possess.

Some ideas are unselfish. Some are self-indulgent. But either way, you've concluded that you can't do any of them because you don't presently have the means to do so.

It's only logical, right? "This is what I've got, so this is what I can do."

A logical calculation, perhaps, but it's not an entirely biblical one.

If you are a believer in Jesus Christ, God has called you to live by a different premise. He has invited you to live beyond your present resources. It's called *faith*.

Humanly we look at what we currently have—whether by way of money, time, energy, gifts, talents, or something else—and then we decide what we are able to do.

Note the words: what *we are able* to do!

Remember, we've already settled on this: *I can't. God can*. But our default thinking only takes in the first half of that conclusion. As followers of Jesus Christ we are called to live not by our ability but by God's ability.

Humanly we look at what we have and decide what we can do. Spiritually we are called to look at what we are called to do and move forward trusting we'll receive from God what we need along the way.

Two competing worldviews collide at the intersection of purpose and resources.

One says, "I have; therefore I can."

The other demands, "I must; therefore I will possess what is necessary."

Talk about two radically different ways to live!

Of course the key is to determine what God calls us each to do. There's a whole conversation wrapped up in that. If you are struggling with knowing God's will, perhaps you'll want to revisit the previous chapter. But let's suffice it to say that in making that decision you are not to start with how much is in your bank account, pocket, or purse. You are to start with God. What resources does God possess that could be brought into the equation?

When we know what God has called us to do and we choose to do it (regardless of whether it appears we can or cannot achieve it), God promises to provide exactly what is needed as we take each step along the way.

The one approach looks at the size of your bank account, the other at the size of your God.

This is a spiritual principle. It is rock solid, enduringly true.

We are tempted, therefore, to apply it only to what we deem to be spiritual circumstances. But as a spiritual principle, it is a *life* principle. It ought, therefore, to be applied to all of life.

There is a grumpy fellow working next to me at the office. He grates on my nerves. Yet I am called to love him in Jesus' name.

Try. Fail. Try. Fail. Try. Fail.

Frustration!

Finally you cry out, "Lord, I can't do this! Give me your love for him. Come love him through me."

That's the right application, but we fail because we leave it there.

We need to see that for a believer, everything is spiritual—not just loving Grumpy Gus at work but also matters like income, houses, cars, budgeting, and the use of our money.

Interestingly, God makes one of His strongest promises in just this context. "God is able to make all grace abound to you, so that having all sufficiency in all things at all times, you may abound in every good work" (2 Cor. 9:8).

Take a gander at all those superlatives: "all," "abound," "all things," "all times," "having all sufficiency," "abound in every good work"!

Let me guess: You're inwardly thinking, "That sounds like health-and-wealth-preacher talk!"

Believe me that's *not* what I'm saying. Listen carefully again. You'll find that this is actually God talk. Your Father is enumerating several principles—like train rails—down which He intends to increase your intimacy with Him, your effectiveness for Him, and your joy in Him.

Let me state five divinely issued principles lifted directly from the pages of God's Word here in 2 Corinthians 9. God left them for you so that you can live life by looking at Him, not at your wallet.

27

REWARD

Are you ready for the first principle? Here it is: *We each choose our own reward.*

"The point is this: whoever sows sparingly will also reap sparingly, and whoever sows bountifully will also reap bountifully" (2 Cor. 9:6).

Everybody sows. Everybody reaps. It is inviolable, unchangeable.

Not everyone sows the same; not all reaping is identical. Some reap "sparingly" and others reap "bountifully."

We each reap as we've sown.

That is true in all of life—not just in the arena of money and giving. That is why Paul could say to the Galatian believers, "Do not be deceived: God is not mocked, for whatever one sows, that will he also reap. For the one who sows to his own flesh will from the flesh reap corruption, but the one who sows to the Spirit will from the Spirit reap eternal life" (Gal. 6:7–8).

So here's what you need to do. Start at your desired end and work backward to the present moment. That is to say, choose what you want to reap. Decide on what reward you wish to receive. Then work your way backward and determine what you need to do now.

A gardener says, "I want huge, juicy tomatoes in August." There is, therefore, something you must do in March. During those dark days of late winter (you can tell where I live), you need to gather some seeds, potting soil, and one of those special grow lights. If you want ripe, red, juicy tomatoes come harvest time, you have to get the plants started in your basement before spring.

A student says, "I want to earn a college degree." If you're in high school your work begins now. Learn how to study. Work to raise your GPA. Talk to a career counselor. Start contacting select schools. If you're done with high school, complete your college application. Start plotting your course work, schedule classes, work on financial aid. You won't walk the aisle to receive your sheepskin if you don't.

We do this in many areas of life but are hesitant to believe it necessary in the spiritual realm. We are even less likely to see the connection in the area of giving of our financial resources.

It's true nevertheless—we each choose our own reward. We do so by our obedience in the area of giving and withholding physical and tangible things. We are hesitant to believe the principle holds true with financial and physical things because we confuse *receiving* with *reward.*

We think, "If I receive it, it must be my reward." We conclude that whatever comes our way is a reward to be used for our enjoyment. It may, however, only be the resource designed to gain you a greater reward. That extra, unexpected cash that's come your way recently may not be a fall harvest, but the delivery of seed in the spring. That is to say, God may have sent it your way not for immediate consumption, but for a faith investment in a greater harvest.

If you confuse the matter of receiving and reward you might be guilty of eating seeds in March rather than tomatoes in August.

What you continue to receive in the future is tied directly to whether you hold on to or release what you've received in the present.

This leads us to the second principle we must embrace: *We choose our reward by our giving.*

There is a direct correlation between sowing and reaping. If you want to reap green beans, you can't plant squash. You want tomatoes? Then you can't plant pole beans.

Reaping is always directly related to sowing. What you want to reap (or experience as a reward) in life here and in eternity is in direct relationship to how you sow (give) in this life.

Sowing sparingly never ends in reaping bountifully.

That makes some of us a bit nervous.

Perhaps you say, "But aren't we saved by grace alone? Isn't the promise that we'll reap a life we have not earned?"

I am eternally delighted to affirm, yes, we are indeed saved by grace alone. Thank God!

We are saved by grace through faith alone. But the same Bible tells us we are rewarded for obedience. Salvation is a gift; rewards are earned. "For we must all appear before the judgment seat of Christ, so that each one may be recompensed for his deeds in the body, according to what he has done, whether good or bad" (2 Cor. 5:10 NASB).

The *fact of relationship* is free. The *future of rewards* will cost you obedience, sacrifice, and service. That is precisely why Erwin Lutzer can say, "The person you are today will determine the rewards you will receive tomorrow."[1]

28

DECISION

Are you ready for a third vital principle? Here it is: *We each make up our own minds about our giving.*

"Each one must give as he has decided in his heart, not reluctantly or under compulsion, for God loves a cheerful giver" (2 Cor. 9:7).

There is to be no arm-twisting, manipulation, or guilt-laden appeals when it comes to fundraising in God's work. Each one is to make his own decision "in his heart."

So don't just respond emotionally. Think things through. Give intentionally with purpose and strategically. Pray about your giving. Predetermine what you will do with your money, what place it will hold in your life, and how you will invest it in worthy efforts to help others and advance God's work.

That doesn't mean giving is disconnected from our emotions. There is to be joy ("cheerful") in the giving. And only grace can motivate joy in giving. Put one eye on God's giving—"For you know the grace of our Lord Jesus Christ, that though he was rich, yet for your sake he became poor, so that you by his poverty might become rich" (2 Cor. 8:9). Then consider how your giving will respond to and reflect His giving.

When it comes to sowing (giving), motive is everything. When "the Lord comes," He "will both bring to light the things hidden in the darkness and disclose the motives of men's hearts; and then each man's praise will come to him from God" (1 Cor. 4:5 NASB). Repeatedly the Scriptures call us to obey God "from the heart."

Being manipulated to give makes it something other than obedience, and God only rewards obedience.

These principles may be starting to pile up in your mind, so let's take a moment to review.

- We each choose our own reward.
- We choose our reward by our giving.
- And we each make up our own minds about our giving.

That is as it should be. But know this as well—we don't have forever to do our giving. We only have so much time to live, and therefore we have only so much time to give.

Willard Cantelon, in his book *The Day the Dollar Dies*, tells of an elderly German woman who survived World War II. As a new era dawned upon her shattered homeland, she heard of a new Bible school that was being started on the outskirts of the bombed out city of Frankfurt. She gladly came forward with an offering to help in the construction and startup costs of the new school. This was money for which she had worked hard. She had worked even harder throughout the war to protect and keep it from the Nazis. Cantelon writes, "She was investing it in a worthy cause and beamed with pride as she offered her contribution." But, as he goes on, he says, "How could I tell her she had held this money too long? Why did it fall my lot to shock this sensitive soul with the news that her money was virtually worthless? Why had she not read the morning paper, or heard the announcement that the new government in Bonn had cancelled this currency?"[1]

That Sunday in June 1948 many Germans committed suicide. Millions lost their life's savings because the German mark had been canceled by the government. Erwin Lutzer, reflecting upon the turn of events said, "If only they had exchanged their money for something that would survive the economic collapse."[2]

It is true we choose our reward by our giving, but we only have this life—*today!*—to prepare our reward.

29

HAVE AND HAVE NOT

Three principles down, two to go. Are you still with me? OK, here then is the fourth principle: *What we currently have should not determine if we can currently give.*

This is so counterintuitive that we need to slow down and carefully think this through. It isn't that we should not give out of what we currently have. Certainly we should. Paul counseled the Corinthian believers to begin their giving with what they already possessed: "For if the readiness is there, it is acceptable according to what a person has, not according to what he does not have" (2 Cor. 8:12).

We begin our giving with what we currently have, but that is not where our giving is to end. God wants to move you into a level of trust and experience wherein your giving need not be bound *only* to what you currently possess.

Quite simply: God can enable you to give beyond your means.

What an odd statement to our Western, materialistic ears! But it's true because, if you determine to trust God, He can provide all you need to accomplish your desired giving. In fact, God promises to do so.

"And God is able to make all grace abound to you, so that having all sufficiency in all things at all times, you may abound in every good work. As it is written, 'He has distributed freely, he has given to the poor; his righteousness endures forever' " (2 Cor. 9:8–9).

Note again those inclusive phrases.

- "all grace"—both spiritual and material/financial
- "all sufficiency"—for both living and giving
- "in all things"—no matter the need
- "all times"—no matter what the stock market says, whether it is a bull market or a bear market; regardless of what your bank account says; in boom or in bust; in recession or progression
- "every good work"—that is required by God

Let's just cut to the chase: Do you want to live daily by God's ability or by your own? Do you want to live in what *God* is able to do rather than always having life defined by what *you* are able to do?

Sadly, we often settle for less. Instead of living in "all grace," we settle for present grace. Instead of "all things," we settle for some things. Instead of at "all times," we settle for some of the time. Rather than "all sufficiency," we make do with a ho-hum experience of God's ability to supply.

Try this: Look at what you have in terms of money and assets. Then ask yourself: Is this *bread,* or is it *seed*? Is all this bread to be consumed, or is some of this seed to be planted? Is it possible that God sent some of this not as my daily bread but as seed to be sown for a future harvest? Is this to be spent, or is it to be invested? Is this for right now, or is this given with hopes of a larger harvest later?

As you embrace and submit to God's mission, what you currently have does not have to be the sole determiner of what you are able to give.

True, in the present moment, you can only give what you have. For heaven's sake don't write a check for which you don't have money in the bank! But that said, the Bible does say, "We walk by faith, not by sight" (2 Cor. 5:7).

The determining factor of what you can give need not be merely what you can currently *see*—whether in your wallet, bank account, assets, or investment portfolio. God promises that you will always have everything you need to obey Him with regard to giving.

The key is not merely determining what you can do with what you have, but what God calls you to do by way of obedience and what He is able to supply you. That is to say (and here's our fifth principle): *As we give, God can multiply what we have.*

"He who supplies seed to the sower and bread for food will supply and multiply your seed for sowing and increase the harvest of your righteousness. You will be enriched in every way to be generous in every way, which through us will produce thanksgiving to God" (2 Cor. 9:10–11).

As we give, God multiplies. On God's calculator the multiply button has not the symbol of an *X* but of an open hand! When God sees one of His own holding loosely to the blessings He's poured into his or her life, He starts multiplying.

The outcome of such calculated giving is not *less* but *more*—both in your own life and in the lives of others. He promises a "harvest of . . . righteousness" (v. 10), and that isn't just (or even primarily) dollars. God guarantees that you "will be enriched in every way" (v. 11), not just monetarily.

By any merely human calculation if you give what is in your hand, it will result in less in your hand . . . and more in someone else's. But God demands, "That is not how my math works."

Never let what you currently have determine your obedience to God.

Amaziah became the king of Judah when just twenty-five years of age. Immediately it seemed his reign was tested. Edom started rattling its saber to test the mettle of this new monarch. Amaziah thus called together his army to prepare for battle (2 Chron. 25:5). But when the king looked upon his ranks, he felt they were woefully undermanned to take on such a formidable foe. He hatched a plan to hire one hundred thousand mercenaries from the northern kingdom of Israel (v. 6). The problem was that Israel was in rebellion against the Lord at the time (v. 7) and would not, therefore, have His blessing. Nevertheless, Amaziah paid out one hundred talents of gold for their military aid.

We are not used to thinking in units of measure such as "talents." Think of it this way—it was the equivalent of seven thousand, five hundred pounds of gold. That's over three-and-a-half tons of gold! On today's market that is the equivalent of roughly $156 million!

"But a man of God came to him and said, 'O king, do not let the army of Israel go with you, for the Lord is not with Israel' " (v. 7).

That had to go down hard for the new king. The prophet went on, "But go, act, be strong for the battle. Why should you suppose that God will cast you down before the enemy? For God has power to help or to cast down" (v. 8).

You can guess Amaziah's first question for the prophet. He asked "the man of God, 'But what shall we do about the hundred talents that I have given to the army of Israel?' " (v. 9).

Yeah! What about the dough? What about the 156 million dollars? He couldn't just walk away from that!

"The man of God answered, '*The Lord is able to give you much more than this*' " (v. 9).

Wait a minute! Don't even think about reading on. Stop and ponder that.

God "is able to give you much more than" 156 million dollars?

Yes.

God is saying to you right now, "Obey me right now—regardless of what the cost appears to be, regardless of whether it appears to be possible or not—and I'll see that you always have what you need both for living and giving."

Work your way again through Paul's logic:

- We each choose our own reward.
- We choose our reward by our giving.
- We each make up our own minds about our giving.
- What we currently have should not determine what we can currently give.
- As we give, God is able to multiply what we have.

30

THE CHECK

The smells and sounds of sizzling pizza filled my senses and awakened the hunger pangs I had been working hard to ignore. The waitress placed before my wife Julie, our small son Joseph, and me the long-awaited meal. We had managed to steal away for a few minutes together over lunch amid the busy schedule of ministry life. This week the treadmill had been turned up a notch; this was day three of our four-day missions conference.

A few bites into our pizza, the screams of my hungry stomach now quieting down, I raised the topic I had been exhorting our church family to discuss for weeks, "What about our Faith Promise?"[1] In our tradition we annually pledge what we plan to give, by God's grace, to the cause of advancing the gospel to the ends of the earth. Julie and I discussed what we had sensed God saying to us individually.

We have always found helpful an old formula for calculating such giving. We begin by answering the question: What *can* we give? It is a matter of looking at our ability, financially speaking. It requires looking at our budget. Having settled that, we then ask a second question: What can we *sacrifice*? Is there something we can cut back on, give up, or find a cheaper solution to, all so that the extra money could go toward funding God's mission to all the peoples of the earth? So we settle that and add it to the first amount. But we're not done until we ask a third question: What can we *trust God to provide*? This is built upon the principles we've discovered in 2 Corinthians 9. If we, as we are led by God, commit to trusting Him for a certain amount of money over the next year—and equally commit to giving it when He provides it—He will gladly, graciously, gloriously do so.

It didn't take us long to work through the first two parts of the formula. But when we came to the question "What can we trust God by faith to provide?" we had to stop for further conversation.

We realized that we'd fallen into a discernable pattern over the past several years. The first year when we added the faith part to our giving, we had no idea where that money would come from. A few months later God faithfully provided exactly what we needed in a way that we would never have expected. What reinforcement to our trust in our Provider!

As the years followed in succession, we continued to include the faith portion in our missions giving. Yet we had to confess that looking back we observed that our faith had turned to presumption. What had, the first year, been an unexpected source of supply had become a regular, almost expected, part of what happened year by year. Our faith had transferred from God to that which at first had only been the means of His provision.

With pizza in hand we resolved that we would continue our faith portion this year. Now, however, we took our eyes off what had become an expectation and put them back on our Provider. He would supply in some way, though we again did not know how.

Later that evening, the restaurant now far behind, we were enjoying a wonderful missions service. A dear, faithful lifelong missionary to the peoples of Peru was speaking at our conference. His text was Psalm 67. He was speaking, but it was God's Spirit who was teaching my heart.

"The earth has yielded its increase; God, our God, shall bless us. God shall bless us; let all the ends of the earth fear him!" (vv. 6–7), he read.

He exhorted us, "Every blessing of God, every provision He sends our way is for the purpose of bringing the peoples of the earth to the fear of God."

With those words the Holy Spirit set my mind in motion: "What had God provided me?" My mind reeled off answers. Indeed, I had been remarkably blessed! But the Spirit seemed to prompt me further: "What had I been blessed with *recently*?"

Suddenly it struck me—the check!

That afternoon Julie had called me at church and asked, "John, are you sitting down?" She had my attention, and it made me nervous. "The mail just came," she said, "and you will never believe what was in it."

All through college and seminary, I had heard of mailbox experiences, but I had never had one myself until that day. We received a rather substantial check from a totally unexpected source.

This story might end like one of those stories of faith you read in a missionary biography, except for the fact that until that moment in the service I had made no connection between the check in the afternoon mail and the promise we had made to God over lunch. All afternoon I had wondered about how our family might use this money.

Now, however, as God's servant spoke His words, God brought the message home to my heart and broke through my dense unfaithfulness. I realized that in two short hours God provided what we had promised Him would go toward supporting those who take the gospel to the world. In fact long before God prompted us to make that step of faith, He had already put in motion the provision to fill that need. "Before they call I will answer; while they are yet speaking I will hear" (Isa. 65:24).

What a delight it was to stand to close that missions service and add, by way of personal testimony, our amen to the message delivered by our brother. God is faithful. Even where faltering, thick, slow faith is present, God is delighted to prove He still honors faith exercised in giving to that which is most upon His heart.[2]

God's mission and purpose is to glorify His name by calling out from the nations a people for Himself. Many good things get attached to the name of God (and some bad ones too). But this is the center, core, and heart of it all—glorifying His name by redeeming lost people and turning them into worshipers. All else is subservient to this. God is able to supply the needs of every person who determines to share with Him that mission and ministry.

PART SEVEN

GOD IS ABLE TO DO MORE THAN YOU THINK

Now to him who is able to do far more abundantly than all that we ask or think, according to the power at work within us, to him be glory in the church and in Christ Jesus throughout all generations, forever and ever. Amen.

Ephesians 3:20–21

31

EXPECTATIONS

How much should we expect from God?

The question goes to the gut of things. An answer requires understanding something about both God's ability and His will, about what God can do and what God is willing to do.

Let's begin with God's ability and work our way back to His willingness.

To put it bluntly: God is able to do *more than you think.*

I can say so because Paul said so. And he said so because God says so: "Now to him who is able to do far more abundantly than all that we ask or think, according to the power at work within us, to him be glory in the church and in Christ Jesus throughout all generations, forever and ever. Amen." (Eph. 3:20–21).

Marvelous!

Truly it is; simply splendid. Enormously, stunningly, spectacularly true.

Yet, admittedly, it would be easy to get hyped up and run off to do daily life with an adrenalin rush of euphoria, but with a noggin devoid of understanding.

Without in the slightest taking anything away from the infinity-reaching breadth of Paul's claim, we must remember that we are obligated to take all God's words in their context. When we pause for even a moment we quickly realize that this is actually just the last phrase of a larger prayer.

Here's the full prayer.

> For this reason I bow my knees before the Father, from whom every family in heaven and on earth is named, that according to the riches of his glory he may grant you to be strengthened with power through his Spirit in your inner being, so that Christ may dwell in your hearts through faith— that you, being rooted and grounded in love, may have strength to comprehend with all the saints what is the breadth and length and height and depth, and to know the love of Christ that surpasses knowledge, that you may be filled with all the fullness of God. Now to him who is able to do far more abundantly than all that we ask or think, according to the power at work within us, to him be glory in the church and in Christ Jesus throughout all generations, forever and ever. Amen. (Eph. 3:14–21)

But then that prayer is part of a whole bolt of cloth that makes up Ephesians 1–3. In the Bible, as in any conversation, context is king or you won't understand a thing! Thus we can't extract two marvelous verses out of their context and slap them across the bumpers of our lives and go tooling down the road of life without ending up with some misplaced expectations.

As you observe the closing lines of the prayer, you will identify them as doxology. That is to say, they are praise directed to God. Doxology is the place where all sound theology delivers its subjects. All true doctrine aims not to create a big head, but worn knees and worshiping hearts. Truth is given to restore us to our original intent—worshipers of the one true God. Truth leads us, to use Wesley's phrase, to become "Lost in wonder, love, and praise."[1]

It is there, bowed in submission at God's feet, that we pour out our praise and learn to rightly calculate our expectations of God.

32

POTENTIAL

Bowed at God's feet in worship, we discover life with Him has potential unimaginable.

We have been trained to measure potential in many different ways. We are told to look at the prospects, figure the odds, and study the trends. We are coached to analyze our temperament, factor in our emotions, calculate our IQ, and survey our experiences.

God tells us, "Here's how you measure the potential of this life": "Now to him who is able to do far more abundantly than all that we ask or think, according to the power at work within us" (Eph. 3:20). Potential is not measured by our ability, but by the Savior who owns us.

Did you notice how the potential of God's work in and through us is telescoped out and extended further and further?

- Him who is *able* . . .
- Him who is able *to do* . . .
- Him who is able to do *more* . . .
- Him who is able to do *far* more . . .
- Him who is able to do far more *abundantly* . . .
- Him who is able to do far more abundantly than *all* . . .

- Him who is able to do far more abundantly that all we *ask* . . .
- Him who is able to do far more abundantly than all we ask or *think*!

Length by length, as if unfolding a vast landscape, Paul extends God's abilities eight different times. I picture it like an extension ladder. You are staring up at that next step of obedience God is calling you to. You've already cried out, "Lord, I can't. It'll never reach!" But section by section, word by word, the apostle reminds you "You're correct. You can't. But God can."

When Paul says God "is able," he uses a present tense verb, which underscores what is continuously true of God. There is never a time when God is not fully able to do all that He wills to do. When he says God is able "to do," he uses an aorist tense, which, though it can have various nuances of meaning, seems to describe here God's actions at specific points in time.[1] God is ever and always—regardless of time, place, people, problems, or something else—able! And He will manifest that ability at any given moment in any given set of circumstances as you trust Him.

God's ability is a line—He is always, enduringly able. God's acts are a dot—He moves in specific moments, at precise times, and in particular events. In the moment, trust God to be all He ever has been and ever will be.

Tozer was right, wasn't he? "Anything God has ever done, He can do now. Anything God has ever done anywhere, He can do here. Anything God has done for anyone else, He can do for you."[2]

As you move into the future, God is going to ask of you steps of obedience that you will conclude are impossible. He will call upon you for acts of service which you will determine are unattainable. He will require of you leadership that you'll tell Him is unrealistic. God will require of you things that are beyond you and which will leave you pleading, "But God, I can't do it."

I can't is a valid argument within the worldview of naturalism. In fact it is the only sane conclusion. And it must, in that case, end in despair. But *I can't* is an invalid argument when you are speaking of the world as it truly is, the world with God, the sovereign Creator and Sustainer of all things, sitting upon His throne. In such a world, it's never about you (or me). It is all about Him.

God consistently hands out assignments designed to bring us to the end of ourselves, and thus to the beginning of His infinite resources. As the great missionary J. Hudson Taylor said, "All God's giants have been weak men who did great things for God because they reckoned on Him being with them."[3]

Did you note that Paul did not say God has the ability to do more "than *you* ask or think"?

No. To quote again, He has the ability to do more "than *we* ask or think." That plural pronoun, of course, brings the great apostle himself into our prayer circle. Just think of what Paul has dared to ask God for already in this letter.

> For this reason, because I have heard of your faith in the Lord Jesus and your love toward all the saints, I do not cease to give thanks for you, remembering you in my prayers, that the God of our Lord Jesus Christ, the Father of glory, may give you the Spirit of wisdom and of revelation in the knowledge of him, having the eyes of your hearts enlightened, that you may know what is the hope to which he has called you, what are the riches of his glorious inheritance in the saints, and what is the immeasurable greatness of his power toward us who believe, according to the working of his great might that he worked in Christ when he raised him from the dead and seated him at his right hand in the heavenly places, far above all rule and authority and power and dominion, and above every name that is named, not only in this age but also in the one to come. And he put all things under his feet and gave him as head over all things to the church, which is his body, the fullness of him who fills all in all. (Eph. 1:15–23)

Or just remember the first part of his prayer here:

> For this reason I bow my knees before the Father, from whom every family in heaven and on earth is named, that according to the riches of his glory he may grant you to be strengthened with power through his Spirit in your inner being, so that Christ may dwell in your hearts through faith— that you, being rooted and grounded in love, may have strength to comprehend with all the saints what is the breadth and length and height and depth, and to know the love of Christ that surpasses knowledge, that you may be filled with all the fullness of God. (Eph. 3:14–19)

My goodness! Clearly Paul is not timid in his ability to ask.

Then consider what Paul has dared *think* in this letter!

He believes that God the Father "put all things under [the glorified Jesus'] feet and gave him as head over all things to the church, which is his body, the fullness of him who fills all in all" (1:22–23). He pictures the church as the fullness "of him who fills all in all."

Stunning!

And he depicts God's purpose for the church in grand terms as well: "So that through the church the manifold wisdom of God might now be made known to the rulers and authorities in the heavenly places" (3:10).

Clearly Paul has a far-ranging concept of God's plan for His people, full of broad vistas of purpose and glory beyond what most any of us would dare dream.

The world says: "If you can dream it, you can achieve it." God replies, "No! It's far more than that."

If you can ask for it, ask again, for God's desire is far beyond that. If you can imagine it, think again, for God's desire for us is well beyond even your wildest dreams.

I've banked on this statement ever since I heard Robertson McQuilkin say it over thirty years ago, "Never underestimate God. Never underestimate God in you!"[4]

God is able. His ability is unlimited and unimaginable to even the brightest of minds and the most faith-filled of hearts.

Staggering! And to think, Paul is just getting warmed up.

33

POWER

Potential is a great thing. Really it is. But without power, potential is a pipedream. Life in Christ is where potential unimaginable meets power unbounded. God "is able to do . . . according to the power at work within us." (Eph. 3:20).

Let's be sure we're clear here. God is not calling you to:

- "Try harder!"
- "Believe in yourself!"
- "Shoot for the stars!"
- "Be all you can be!"
- "Live up to your potential!"

Who is the focus of all these mantras and philosophies? *You!*

If there was ever anything limited, it's you and me. Can we be better than we are? Sure. Can we ever be what we ought? Not without Christ.

All these wild, unthinkable things God may call you to . . . how are they going to become reality?

Everything you need to do the unimaginable and unprayable is already present in your life, if you are a follower of Christ. You don't need something you don't have. The truth is God desires something He may not yet have—your yielded willingness to obey Him no matter what He requires.

Glance again at Paul's great prayer in Ephesians 1. You'll notice that he piles one word atop another as he inventories God's ability: "power," "working," "great might," "worked" (vv. 19–20).

Ask yourself, to what end is this power given? For the doing of wild exploits for God? Perhaps, as God may call. But God's primary point in making available this power is that we might become the right kind of people, long before we worry too much about doing outlandish feats for God.

Later in this same letter Paul will command us to "be filled with the Spirit" (Eph. 5:18). To what end? Not to produce a *what*, but a *who*! For immediately he describes what such Spirit-filled believers look like. They are fervent worshipers (vv. 19–20), submissive wives (vv. 22–24), sacrificially loving husbands (vv. 25–33), obedient children (6:1–3), patient, loving fathers (v. 4), faithful servants (vv. 5–8), and just employers (v. 9).

This unbounded power is given more that we might *be* the right kind of people than simply that we might *do* the right kinds of things. As we prioritize becoming the right kind of people, God provides the power to make us just that—transforming us as wives, husbands, children, parents, employees, and employers. At that point the world stands up to take notice.

What would such possibilities mean to married people crying, "I can't live like this any longer"? To parents despairing, "I can't take one more day"? To children who think, "I can't stand my parents"? To employees on Sunday night despondent over the coming work week, confessing, "I'll die if I have to go back there one more day"?

It would offer the greatest gift one person can offer another—hope.

So as we live in relationship with God, we embrace a life that has potential unimaginable and power unbounded. But even that isn't the end.

34
PURPOSE

Potential without power is a wisp of vapor. Potential infused with unbounded power becomes something unimaginable. But power and potential get together only at the launching pad of purpose. God does not just give His power away for no reason. Find God's purpose and you'll find God's power to live within divine potential.

What is God's purpose? That God will receive "glory in the church and in Christ Jesus throughout all generations, forever and ever" (Eph. 3:21).

Our purpose is the glory of God. It is our purpose because it is our Creator's purpose. Our purpose is not found amid our preferences, likes, dislikes, comfort, tastes, or style. Our purpose is not our dreams, plans, visions, wishes, or agendas.

Everything is always about the glory of God. The glory of God is the goal—of everything. This is a purpose unequalled by anything, anyone, anywhere, at any time.

Why did God, who resided from all eternity in the intimate, perfect fellowship of the Trinity, choose to create this world and the human race? Why did Lucifer choose to leave his appointed station and covet the place that belongs to God alone? Why does he fight and wage war still, though he knows he is a defeated foe? Why did Jesus die, rise, and commit the progress of the divine redemptive plan to the hands of eleven men?

It's pretty simple, really. To demonstrate the greatness of His glory as a giver.

Whatever is at issue, the ultimate issue is always and ultimately the glory of God.

Dr. David Rambo, former president of The Christian and Missionary Alliance, once said, "Isn't it good to be involved in something bigger than ourselves . . . and to be into something which is so formidable and so challenging that all we can say as we gurgle down [is], 'Save me, Lord, or I perish'? This living dangerously . . . is a great thing. It is great to be alive at such a time as this."[1]

Everything about everything is about the glory of God!

All of it. The answered prayers and the unanswered prayers. Christ's redemption, death, resurrection, and session. The Holy Spirit given. The church sent. You placed in your particular neighborhood, family, workplace, school, home, and church.

Think of all God has done for the purpose of simply displaying His glory. Everything God the Father has done in redemption is "to the praise of his glorious grace" (Eph. 1:6). Everything the Son has done in leaving heaven, living on earth, redeeming us at the cost of His life, was to purchase for Himself a people who "might be to the praise of his glory" (v. 12). The Holy Spirit's ministry is to bring us into the fullness of our inheritance "to the praise of his glory" (v. 14).

Look again at Ephesians 3:21 even more carefully this time. God will find His glory *where*? "In the church and in Christ Jesus."

He didn't say "in John Kitchen, his ministry, his family, his short life."

I, like you, tend to read this in an individualistic way. It is just about the only way we know to read anything as Americans. But for that very reason we often misread and misapply Scripture.

Yes, your life and mine are included in this, but not as the ends. It just isn't all about you or me. It is about *us*. It is about *we*. It is about you and me and us all being "the church." It is about us living in relationship. It is about us corporately living together as the visible expression of "Christ Jesus" in this world.

Christ is our (not *my*!) Head. We (not *I*!) are His body!

How do we know this is the emphasis here? Well, what are the next words?

Remember, the chapter breaks and verse numbers were only to give these things an address where we could quickly find them; they are not part of the Bible's original text.

So with the same breath Paul uses to tell us that in Christ we live in potential unimaginable, power unbounded, and a purpose unequaled, he immediately says, "I therefore, a prisoner for the Lord, urge you to walk in a manner worthy of the calling to which you have been called" (Eph. 4:1).

And what, we may ask, does such a calling require? What does it look like?

It is to live with one another "with all humility and gentleness, with patience, bearing with one another in love, eager to maintain the unity of the Spirit in the bond of peace" (Eph. 4:2–3).

It is to live knowing "There is one body" that is given life by "one Spirit." It is to look around and realize together we "were called to the one hope that belongs to your call." It is to know that we serve "one Lord," ascribe to "one faith," and all alike entered into "one baptism." We bow together under "one God" and together look to one "Father of all, who is over all and through all and in all" (vv. 4–6).

No, we haven't lost our individuality. Yes, God has given "grace . . . to each one of us" (v. 7) as individuals. But that was not for our own enjoyment, but "for building up the body of Christ" (v. 12). And it was for the purpose that "we *all* attain to the unity of the faith and of the knowledge of the Son of God, to mature manhood, to the measure of the stature of the fullness of Christ" (v. 13).

I could go on, but just keep reading the rest of Ephesians 4 and you'll see that God's plan is to glorify Himself in the church.

But let your eyes wander back to chapter 3 and verse 21. Does it bother you that, in describing God's plan to bring glory to Himself, Paul put the church ahead of Jesus Christ?

It seems to have bothered the early copyists of the New Testament, because it wasn't long before they began revising it by reversing the order. They, it appears, wondered that the apostle would give Jesus second billing. "What's with that?"

If you carefully read Ephesians you'll notice that the church and Christ are almost not (and I must be careful with my wording here to avoid misstatement) even considered separate entities. He is the head, and we are His body.

No, I'm not talking ontological oneness—as if we become divine or that Jesus becomes indistinguishable from His people. But I'm simply saying that God has so brought us as His people into union with His Son that we are "the body of Christ" (4:12) and Jesus is our Head (v. 15).

Even apart from all that rather mystical spiritual truth, who gives you the most worry when it comes to bringing glory to God? Christ? Or the church?

One commentator puts it this way, "The honour of Jesus is in the hands of the Church."[2]

That is a high and holy calling, my friends. This is what Paul has been telling us throughout these first three chapters of Ephesians.

35

DURATION

How long will the glory of God be our purpose? It will last "throughout all generations, forever and ever" (Eph. 3:21). Never will you have any other purpose; never will our high calling fall away; never will we be free to pursue another purpose.

To this Paul adds his solemn amen. As we have already seen, the word means something like "truly!" or "may it be so."

Amen has, in some corners, become a trite word. In others it has come to signal little more than intellectual assent to something.

But our amen must mean more than this. It is wholehearted, faith-filled, passionate affirmation that reaches out and lays hold of the truth and says, "Yes! Yes! This is what I want too!"

So let me ask, does this potential unimaginable, this power unbounded, this purpose unequaled rise up in your heart till it must cry amen? Are you willing to take these as the marching orders and reality-defining boundaries of your life? Will you take these over personal comfort, personal tastes, preferences, desires, opinions?

Hear Tozer once again, "Brethren, we have been born of God and our Christian hope is a valid hope! No emptiness, no vanity, no dreams that cannot come true. Your expectation should rise and you should challenge God and begin to dream high dreams of faith and spiritual attainment and expect God to meet them. You cannot out-hope God and you cannot out-expect God. Remember that all of your hopes are finite, but all of God's ability is infinite!"[1]

So, coming, full circle let me ask again: What should we expect from God?

Yes, life with God includes potential unimaginable, power unbounded, purpose unequaled. But how do I match these with my expectations of Him in this life?

Philip Yancey begins his book *Disappointment with God*, with honest words: "I found that for many people there is a large gap between what they *expect* from their Christian faith and what they actually experience. From a steady diet of books, sermons, and personal testimonies, all promising triumph and success, they learn to expect dramatic evidence of God working in their lives. If they do not see such evidence, they feel disappointment, betrayal, and often guilt."[2]

Where do the heightened expectations of Scripture's promises and the hard realities of life in this fallen world kiss?

Here is what I've concluded. In Christ we enjoy a potential unimaginable *because* God promises a power which is unbounded *because* we've been given a purpose that is unequaled. Read the conjunctions carefully! The conjunction "because" connects the dots and leads us to clarified expectations.

In fact, let me present it to you as an Expectation Calculator. There are two possible ways to calculate our expectations of God in this life.

The first is this: Forsake the purpose—lose the power—forfeit the potential. The sum is always disappointment.

The second is this: Embrace the purpose—experience the power—realize the potential. This always adds up to joy!

We live stunted, diminished lives because we've chosen to pursue feeble, self-serving purposes. God just doesn't give His power away for such pursuits. But when we embrace God's purpose as our own—and let there be no misunderstanding, this will require death to self—we then discover a life that is bigger, grander, and richer than any we ever dreamed. Decide which kind of life you want to live. Then work your way back to the determined choice of the purpose for which you must live.

Life with God has potential unimaginable precisely because it has power unbounded precisely because it embraces a purpose unequaled. If this is true, then the future is not exactly like what you see in your head right now, will not be comfortable, and will not primarily be about you.

It means that if I am to *embrace* the future God desires to give me, then I must *release* to God the picture of the future I hold in my mind right now, *confirm* to God that I will never measure my choices by what I can do, and *commit* to God that I will let my personal preferences and tastes go.

PART EIGHT

GOD IS ABLE TO GUARD YOU

But I am not ashamed, for I know whom I have believed, and I am convinced that he is able to guard until that day what has been entrusted to me.

2 Timothy 1:12

36

GOD ON GUARD

God guards the one who guards the gospel.

It was a Tuesday, shortly after the new school year had begun, August 20, 2013 to be exact. A man carrying an AK-47 assault rifle and packing five hundred rounds of ammunition walked into the Ronald E. McNair Discovery Learning Center in Atlanta, Georgia.

He had come to kill kids.

He also fully expected—maybe even hoped—to see his own life end in a hail of gunfire with the police officers he knew would respond.

The first person he met as he came through the door was Antoinette Tuff, a school clerk. Antoinette saw the murderous look in his eyes and calmly engaged him in conversation, allowing the other school leaders to guide the children out of the school and to safety. When asked by an ABC News reporter about what went through her mind at that moment, she told of a recent sermon series her pastor had begun preaching and how she began to pray for the young man. She told the story of God's grace in her own life. She told the troubled young man she loved him.

The interviewer told her, "You're the hero today." Antoinette replied, "I give it all to God. I'm not the hero. I was terrified." The reporter observed, "You kept it together." Antoinette again rebuffed any personal credit, saying, "Through His grace and mercy I did."[1]

Because of her actions and God's grace that enabled them, everyone—all the children, all the teachers and school leaders, Antoinette, even the gunman himself—survived that day.

What an awesome story! It makes me want to shout, "Yes!" It's almost enough to make you want to break out in the refrain of that old hymn:

> I know whom I have believed,
> And am persuaded that He is able
> To keep that which I've committed
> Unto Him against that day.[2]

But earlier that same day, half a world away, Islamic extremists slipped into the tiny Nigerian village of Dumba in the predawn hours. They slit the throats of forty-four Christians and then gouged out the eyes of many who had watched as their family, friends, and neighbors were butchered.[3]

How's that go again?

> I know whom I have believed,
> And am persuaded that He is able
> To keep that which I've committed
> Unto Him against that day.[4]

Tell me again how exactly does that work?

The song is based on a great statement by a dedicated Christian who was soon to die . . . and knew it. He would die not just by getting his throat slit, but by having his head removed entirely from his body. Yet still he said, "I know whom I have believed and am persuaded that He is able to keep what I have committed to Him until that Day" (2 Tim. 1:12, NKJV).

God will guard those who trust Him. So says the great apostle!

And you've got to admit, it sounds great. It certainly makes for a great hymn.

But what exactly does it mean?

It does not mean that Christians won't suffer, for the theme of Paul's entire paragraph is suffering for the gospel (vv. 8–12). Nor does it mean we won't face martyrdom for Christ, for Paul knew he soon would.

If it doesn't mean that, what does it mean?

Did the faith of Paul and the Nigerian believers fail to measure up to that of the school clerk in Atlanta?

No, God's promise is equally true for Paul, the Nigerian believers, and Antoinette Tuff.

It still stands true: *God guards the one who guards the gospel.*

But that leaves us with some questions, doesn't it?

37

GUARDING THE GOSPEL

Let's start our questions here: *What does it mean to guard the gospel?*

It is always helpful to remember that any sentence of Scripture is made in a particular context. This sentence by the apostle Paul is no different, and if we wish to understand it, we must understand it in the context of all he was saying.

Two verses later Paul told Timothy, "By the Holy Spirit who dwells within us, guard the good deposit entrusted to you" (2 Tim. 1:14). Just a page before this in your Bible he had exclaimed, "O Timothy, guard the deposit entrusted to you" (1 Tim. 6:20).

Clearly God lays on us the responsibility to guard the gospel. It is an imperative. God issues it as a command. This is not left to us as an option, a talking point, or as something to mull over and decide about at a later time.

The Greek word here means to "put on deposit." It was a technical term in the first century world to describe putting money, important documents, or even a will on deposit for safe keeping. Often this was done at the local pagan temple, which served as the equivalent to our modern banks. Or perhaps you could entrust the items to a faithful friend for safekeeping.[1]

It was somewhat akin to our modern Federal Deposit Insurance Corporation. The FDIC was created in 1933 in response to the thousands of bank failures across the nation which plunged millions of

Americans into economic ruin. The FDIC guarantees your deposit up to a quarter of a million dollars.

Or picture a fallen, dying soldier on the battlefield. His comrade in arms comes to his side and seeks to comfort him. But the dying man tells him, "There is a letter in my coat pocket. Please make sure my wife gets it." That soldier feels the weight of that responsibility fall upon him, and he tucks the letter in his own coat and promises his fading friend that he will make sure she receives the letter.

When you hear the gospel of Jesus Christ, God makes a deposit in your life. You are then responsible to guard and keep that deposit. God Himself will personally hold you responsible for its safekeeping.

Now, another question: *What is this gospel we must guard?*

Paul's entire paragraph answers the question with various descriptive terms. Listen in and then let's circle back to note those gospel expressions.

> Therefore do not be ashamed of the testimony about our Lord, nor of me his prisoner, but share in suffering for the gospel by the power of God, who saved us and called us to a holy calling, not because of our works but because of his own purpose and grace, which he gave us in Christ Jesus before the ages began, and which now has been manifested through the appearing of our Savior Christ Jesus, who abolished death and brought life and immortality to light through the gospel, for which I was appointed a preacher and apostle and teacher, which is why I suffer as I do. But I am not ashamed, for I know whom I have believed, and I am convinced that he is able to guard until that day what has been entrusted to me. (2 Tim. 1:8–12)

What is this gospel which God has put on deposit with us?

It is "the testimony about our Lord" (v. 8), the divinely inspired accounts of the life, death, burial, and resurrection of Jesus.

It is, simply, "the gospel" (v. 8). The word means "good news." It is the glad news of Christ's triumph over sin, Satan, and the world. It is the news that God, through Christ, has "saved us" (v. 9). He has saved us from the guilt and penalty of sin, is saving us from sin's power over us, and one day completely will deliver us from sin's very presence. He has saved us from the power of Satan, who used our sin as legal ground to claim us as his own. Jesus saved us from death, from hell, and from wasting the life God has given us.

The gospel tells us that God has "called us with a holy calling" (v. 9 NKJV). When you hear the gospel, God is calling to you—away from life as you have defined it to life as He has designed it. The gospel discloses to us God's own "purpose and grace" (v. 9).

The gospel calls you into a life of purpose. This is a purpose which God Himself designed and "gave us in Christ Jesus before the ages began." This purpose was established before you existed and it resides outside of you and your wishes and dreams. It calls to you. The gospel is the good news that all of this is extended to us free of charge; it is by "grace" and "not because of our works" (v. 9).

The gospel is the glad news that Christ has "abolished death" (v. 10). When Jesus rose from the dead, He defeated death and "destroy[ed] the one who has the power of death, that is, the devil" and delivered "all those who through fear of death were subject to lifelong slavery" (Heb. 2:14–15). In so doing Jesus "brought life and immortality to light through the gospel" (2 Tim. 1:10)!

I'm not sure whether you realize it or not, but God, through these printed words of Scripture, has just put this gospel on deposit with you. Perhaps you have heard it before; maybe not. Either way, God now holds you accountable to guard this gospel. The implications are profound and eternal.

38

HOW TO GUARD THE GOSPEL INWARDLY

Questions remain. So we now ask: *How are we to guard the gospel?*

What did Paul say? "I am not ashamed, for I know whom I have believed, and I am convinced that he is able to guard until that day what has been entrusted to me" (2 Tim. 1:12).

We must guard the gospel inwardly or personally. Paul describes this in a telescoping sequence of faith.

First, we must *believe* the gospel. To believe is to entrust yourself entirely to someone or to something with confidence.

Early this summer, as our church was between youth pastors, I decided to join our teens on their annual trip to Cedar Point, the famous amusement park. There I rode a torture device known as the Top Thrill Dragster. The ride lasts all of fifteen seconds, the first four of which take you from 0 to 120 miles per hour. Waiting in line, there was plenty of time to watch the ride take off and return safely many times, over and over. But I must say that as I sat down in the car, pulled the locking safety yoke over my head, and watched the light countdown to take off, I had the distinct sense that I had entrusted my entire self to something! I simply believed I could ride this thing without dying.

We all live by faith every day. Chances are that this very day you have undertaken a whole series of activities by faith. This morning at some point you swung your feet out of bed and stood up with faith that your legs would indeed hold you upright rather than deposit you in a pile upon the floor. You perhaps have driven a car this very day, speeding down the road and at some point applying your foot to the brake pedal with every confidence that this mass being thrown down the road at such high speed would appropriately and safely come to a resting position. Unless you're standing up as you read, you've rested the entire weight of your body on something. I am assuming that since your eyes are still moving across the page, whatever it is has supported your weight.

All of these activities—and many more—you have undertaken by *faith*. You believed that they would respond as anticipated.

We believe the gospel when we turn from our attempts at self-rule and deliver our entire selves over to Jesus Christ to be ruled by Him as Lord.

We believe. This is imperative. But we must also be *convinced* regarding the gospel and the Savior it holds forth.

To be convinced is "to attain certainty in reference to something."[1]

That Top Thrill Dragster, like almost everything else in life, is subject to the law of diminishing returns. That is to say that the thrill you experience the thirtieth time you ride it is not the same level of excitement as the first time you rode it.

This is not a bad thing. It simply proves that what you believed the first time you rode it (that you would indeed survive the ordeal) has proven in your experience to be true, over and over again. You believed, but now you are *convinced*.

The reason you've undertaken all those various activities today without any real anxiety is that you've done them before, probably many times. You do them now without even thinking, for you have both believed and become convinced of the safety of undertaking them.

Paul opened this very letter by recounting the genuineness of the faith of Timothy's mother and grandmother (2 Tim. 1:5). He then used the same Greek verb he employed in verse 12 ("I am . . . convinced") to tell Timothy "I am sure [that this faith] dwells in you as well." The apostle had seen genuine faith in Timothy's grandmother Lois and his mother Eunice. Now, over time, having walked many miles with Timothy, having seen him under pressure, Paul is utterly convinced of the genuineness of Timothy's faith as well.

Later he will call upon Timothy to "continue in the things you have learned and become convinced of" (3:14, NASB).

So too we guard the gospel when we believe it and continue in it, by our obedience giving God the opportunity to keep His word again and again in our lives, until we are utterly convinced of the truth of this gospel and the Savior who secured it for us.

This, however, is not the end. We must believe and become convinced of the gospel, but ultimately this brings us to the place where we *know* that Jesus and His offer of life are true and reliable. The particular verb Paul uses here stresses the completeness or certainty of the knowledge in view.[2]

By your tenth trip to the amusement park and the fiftieth time you've ridden the ride, you know that all will be well as you strap in and take off. You have come, through repeated experience, to certainty and a deep, pragmatic knowledge of this fact.

Believe. Convinced. Know.

We guard the gospel inwardly and personally as we believe, become convinced, and utterly know that Jesus Christ is true and that His promises are good.

Yet just what is it we are to believe, be convinced of, and know?

That God *is able*!

The word speaks of God's available power. He has strength ready to be delivered at any point we need it. In this case it is power to guard, keep, and protect.

But just *what* does God guard?

39

HOW TO GUARD THE GOSPEL OUTWARDLY

I'm not sure if you noticed or not, but I've already quoted 2 Timothy 1:12 from two different translations, which are nearly identical except for one key phrase. Here they are side by side. I'll highlight the key difference.

> I know whom I have believed, and I am convinced that he is able to guard until that day *what has been entrusted to me.* (ESV)

> I know whom I have believed and am persuaded that He is able to keep *what I have committed to Him* until that Day. (NKJV)

On the one hand God is said to guard something I've put on deposit with Him (NKJV). On the other hand He is said to guard something He's put on deposit with me (ESV).

So which is it?

In both cases these are the translators' best attempt to render a very concise Greek expression that is simply and literally: "my deposit."

Seems simple enough, but by "my deposit" does Paul mean something I've put on deposit with God?[1] This would presumably refer to my life, ministry, service, rewards. Or does it refer to what God has put on deposit with me? This, it would seem, refers to the gospel itself.

In answer I remind you that the context has already made abundantly clear that God holds us accountable for guarding the gospel (1 Tim. 6:20; 2 Tim. 1:14).

That being said, in the present case the one making the deposit seems to have changed, as has the one doing the guarding. For this reason I think the assertion here is that God will keep what Paul entrusts to him. Or to put it more simply, *God guards the one who guards the gospel.*

It is true—we must guard the gospel inwardly by believing it, testing it by our obedience until we are convinced and know in the depth of our being that Jesus and His gospel are true.

But we must also guard the gospel outwardly, or perhaps we could say ministerially. Just before the confident assertion of 2 Timothy 1:12, Paul said it was the gospel (v. 10) "for which [he] was appointed a preacher and apostle and teacher" (v. 11).

We guard the gospel outwardly when we *announce* it. That is what a preacher does. He is a herald, proclaiming a message from the King! It is not time for dialogue, debate, or question-and-answer. The King has something to say and the preacher is His herald to make it known.

We guard the gospel outwardly when we *defend* it. Paul was appointed, for the gospel's sake, as an apostle. It is the gospel of Jesus Christ, but it is given to us through the words and writings of the apostles and their associates. It is the gospel of Jesus Christ, but it is the apostolic gospel. The gospel is not a malleable, soft lump of clay to be formed into whatever we wish it to be. It has specific truth content. It must be defined and defended according to the authoritative word of the apostles as sent out by Jesus Himself.

And we guard the gospel outwardly when we *expound* it. This is the job of the teacher. He unfolds it for his students. Now is the time for dialogue, question-and-answer, exploring the implications, making clarifications, correcting misunderstandings, urging full integration into mind, heart, and life.

Announce. Defend. Expound.

This is Christ's plan for guarding the gospel from one person to another, from one generation to another. The word "guard" shows up again in a slightly different form just a few pen strokes down the page (v. 14). Paul then unfolded for Timothy the divine plan for guarding the gospel when he told him, "what you have heard from me in the presence of many witnesses *entrust* to faithful men, who will be able to teach others also" (2 Tim. 2:2).

Do you see it?

There is the deposit made by Paul in the life of Timothy.

Then there is the deposit made by Timothy in the lives of "faithful men."

Then there is the deposit made by those "faithful men" in the lives of "others also."

Four generations. Four times the passing of the gospel baton. Each time God is underscoring for us that we guard the gospel best, not when we hide it away, but when we *give it away*.

Believe, convinced, know . . . to the point that you announce, defend, and teach. Everlastingly from one life to another, until "that day" breaks upon us and our Savior appears. Do this no matter what it costs, even in the face of suffering (2 Tim. 1:8, 12). Do this "by the power of God" (v. 8) through "the Holy Spirit who dwells in us" (v. 14).

40

GOD GUARDS US

This is all very helpful, but there's one great question remaining: *In what way then does God guard us?*

Paul's life, service, and eternity had been entrusted to God. He believed, was convinced, and knew that his sins were forgiven, that his service was not in vain, and that God's welcome awaited him after death. What did Paul believe, hold as a conviction, and know about how God guards His own?

God guards us not just *from* suffering, but *in* and *through* suffering. Paul called Timothy to "share in suffering for the gospel" (2 Tim. 1:8). He said that being appointed as a preacher, apostle, and teacher of the gospel "is why I suffer as I do" (v. 12).

When Antoinette Tuff faced off with that deranged young man bent on killing children, she told him about her own life, about the hardships she'd faced, about how her heart was broken recently when her husband of thirty-three years walked out on her. Antoinette would be the first to tell you that Jesus had not guarded her from all suffering, though He did guard her that day (and through her, hundreds of others) from death.

John Piper reminds us that suffering is not merely something you may encounter as you guard the gospel, but that suffering is the God-appointed means of advancing the gospel. He tells us, "God intends for the afflictions of Christ to be presented to the world through the afflictions of his people."[1]

God guards us not just *today*, but until "*that day*" (v. 18).

Paul told Timothy that God "is able to guard until that day" what we have entrusted to Him (v. 12).

He seems, in this last of his letters, to have a fixation on "that day." Just a few words later he recounts the faithful service of one Onesiphorus. He had apparently died in service to the Lord. Paul wished that "the Lord grant him to find mercy from the Lord on that day!" (v. 18).

As he draws his letter to a close and bids farewell to Timothy, he says "there is laid up for me the crown of righteousness, which the Lord, the righteous judge, will award to me on that day" (2 Tim. 4:8).

Paul reminds us all that this present moment—whatever it may contain for good or ill—is not the finish line. This present moment is too soon for final deductions to be made.

Presumably this present moment does not also hold your last breath, your last heartbeat, your last brainwave. That is to say, this moment is not the end of you. But there will be a moment when your respirations end, your heart ceases beating, and your brain stops functioning. Will that be the end? Well, yes, of this life; but not of your existence. That moment may be the end of this present life, but it is just the beginning of a fuller entrance into the eternal life Jesus promises us through the gospel.

God guards us not in *shame*, but in *confidence*.

Paul called upon Timothy to "not be ashamed of the testimony of the Lord" (2 Tim. 1:8). He could himself testify, "I am not ashamed" (v. 12).

This is an echo of what he had so boldly declared five or six years earlier when he penned the letter to the Christians in Rome: "I am not ashamed of the gospel, for it is the power of God for salvation to everyone who believes" (Rom. 1:16).

"Ah," you say, "but that was before he was nearly killed by angry mobs in Jerusalem and then arrested. It was before he spent two years in prison in Caesarea, mired in the bureaucracy of the Roman legal system. This was before he had to appeal to Caesar to save his own life. It was before the fateful sea voyage to Rome which included a shipwreck that, apart from divine intervention, would have claimed not only his own life but the lives of all those who sailed with him. That was before he spent an additional two years under house arrest in Rome, awaiting trial. This was before he was eventually released and then ultimately rearrested. This was before this present, much more demanding, second Roman imprisonment. This was prior to the preliminary hearing in which it became clear to him that the die had been cast and he would pay for the gospel with his life."

True. Yet even now—on the other side of all that—he can say, "I am not ashamed, and you ought not to be either."

God guards us not by our *weakness*, but by His *power*.

By now we've established that I can't, but God can. It shouldn't surprise us then that Paul echoes that refrain here at the end of his life. He called Timothy to join him in "suffering for the gospel by the power of God" (2 Tim. 1:8). He reminded Timothy that we can only guard the gospel "by the Holy Spirit who dwells within us" (v. 14).

Thus we can see that God guards the one who guards the gospel.

Simple enough. But mystery abounds in the white space between those letters!

Joni Eareckson Tada, in her book *A Place for Healing: Wrestling with the Mysteries of Suffering*, wrestles again with the events that put her in a wheelchair as a quadriplegic for the last forty years. It is a masterful depiction of God's truth regarding His sovereignty and our suffering, healing, and hope.

Toward the end of the book Joni tells two stories that send rays of divine wisdom shining through what have been long, painful, and challenging years.

The first is the account of an eighteen-year-old woman named Shantamma. Born to an impoverished Hindu family in India, Shantamma was also born with severely malformed legs. She spent her first eighteen years of life pulling herself around on the floor of the family's tiny home, only rarely venturing beyond their front door.

Somehow the pastor of a Bible-believing church made contact with her family and paid them a visit in their home. There he met Shantamma and saw her challenges. He beat a path back to the church, rifled through stacks of books and pulled out a dog-eared copy of an old book titled, simply, *Joni*. The pastor promptly returned to Shantamma's home and presented it to her. Though a Hindu, Shantamma devoured the book. With tears she determined to trust in Jesus Christ "just like Joni."[2] In fact she read and reread the book eight times, seeking to carefully discern how a person could come to salvation in Christ. And this she did. She gave herself in faith to Jesus. It was a decision which bore difficult consequences within her social and religious world.

Four years later, a team from a ministry called Wheels for the World arrived in Shantamma's town ready to hand out wheelchairs for those in need and to fit them to their specific needs. Shantamma was thrilled, after almost two decades of life, to finally receive her very own wheelchair. But when she realized that the chair came from "her very own Joni, from so far away," she was stunned with joy. She told one of the team members, "I am ready to go wherever God leads me in this wheelchair . . . *just like Joni*."[3]

Reflecting upon Shantamma's life, Joni now expresses gratitude to God for *not* healing her of her paralysis. Joni contemplates what may have come to pass had God answered her prayers for healing over forty years before. Teenage prayers, answered by God, might have returned her to what most call a normal life and would have made her an ambulatory adult. But would what she deemed good have been good for Shantamma? Joni begins working through the logic of the events that have transpired in the wake of God *not* answering her prayers as she thought He should. Had God granted her healing, there never would have been a book about her life. So the pastor would have been unable to hand that book to an otherwise hopeless little girl. Joni and Friends and Wheels for the World would not have existed to share wheelchairs to the poor in Shantamma's hometown in India.

Joni sums up God's dealings with her this way: "I only know that because I wasn't healed, because God had plans for my life that were wider and higher and deeper and more profound that I could have ever imagined, a teenage girl named Shantamma from the slums of urban India will be with me in heaven."[4]

Then there was the day that Joni and her friends checked into a hotel after she had spoken at a school for the physically disabled. The housekeeper who had prepared her room (and must have known for whom it was reserved) left a note on the hotel notepad. The note said she had read *Joni* in 1980 shortly after becoming a follower of Christ and that it had been used by God to help her through some of her lowest points.

Joni had noticed when they entered her room that the room next door was still being cleaned. She wondered if it could be the same woman who penned the note. So, wheeling herself next door and through the open door, Joni asked if the woman had left the note for her in the next room.

The woman working inside looked up, saw who asked the question, grabbed a pillow off the bed, buried her face in it, and began to sob. When she was able to compose herself she told Joni that her name was Rachel. She had read Joni's first book and had seen the movie made from it. She told Joni how God had used it as a powerful blessing in her life at a vulnerable time.

Again Joni reflects upon what all these years and what these selective stories from among many others mean to her.

> I . . . know that when God chose not to heal me, He was seeing little Rachel in His mind's eye, loving her, and wanting to provide for her and comfort her heart. And He was seeing Shantamma, who was wondering if anyone in the world could ever help her or care for her as she dragged herself around her little house in Ongole. And He was seeing thousands, perhaps millions of others whom I will never meet on this side of heaven, whose lives were somehow touched by the story of a paralyzed girl in her wheelchair.
>
> And thinking of that, I am filled with awe, and say again, "Thank you, God, for this wheelchair."[5]

We safely may conclude that God is guarding us in a larger, wider, higher, deeper manner than we probably ever dream of. For as we guard the gospel, God guards us, not always from suffering in this life, but always from wasting this life.

He guarded Joni in a mysterious way that we can never quite—this side of heaven—understand. And through her God guarded not only the gospel, but Shantamma and Rachel and thousands, perhaps even millions, more.

On "that day" He will make clear to you that no matter what the gospel may have cost you, He has guarded you for guarding it.

PART NINE

GOD IS ABLE TO GET YOU HOME

Now to him who is able to keep you from stumbling and to present you blameless before the presence of his glory with great joy, to the only God, our Savior, through Jesus Christ our Lord, be glory, majesty, dominion, and authority, before all time and now and forever. Amen.

Jude 1:24–25

41

THE POWER OF HOME

Do you ever wonder if you're going to make it?

Do you despair that you may fail? That you don't have what it takes to fulfill the life you're supposed to live? Do you ever fear you'll just give up and walk away?

I think of how Diana Nyad must have felt. I type these lines just two days after Diana achieved her lifelong dream. At age sixty-four on her fifth attempt to do so, she swam without the aid of a shark cage the 110 miles from Cuba to Florida. It took her fifty-three hours.

It was utterly amazing.

It was a hard-fought achievement that was a long time coming. Diana had made her first attempt thirty-five years before at the age of twenty-nine. She tried again, twice, in 2011. Again she went after her goal in 2012. But finally—and appropriately on Labor Day—Diana walked out of the Florida surf successful.

Simply amazing!

But my concern here is not swimming. I'm talking about something more foundational. The questions I'm posing probe matters of weightier significance than even a personal quest or dream. I'm not even talking about matters as heavy as your marriage, family, career, or physical life. I'm thinking of something more foundational than even those things.

I'm talking about where you stand with God.

Can you make it? Will you make it?

In this spiritually hostile world, a million threats launch themselves at you screaming, "No, you won't!"

It's easy to believe them, isn't it?

I want to close this brief journey of ours by holding out to you a very specific promise God makes to you. As you might expect by now, it is encouraging because it is based upon His ability, not yours.

I can't, but God can. This is the good news we've been probing. We've observed that God is able to

- save you through Jesus Christ,
- establish you in faith in Christ,
- deliver you from all temptation through Christ,
- keep His promises to you in Christ,
- supply your needs through Christ,
- do more than you think through Christ's indwelling presence, and
- guard you as you guard the gospel of Christ.

But can He get you *home*?

That's the great question, isn't it?

In 1914, Sir Earnest Shackleton set out for Antarctica with a full crew of men aboard a ship named—appropriately enough—*Endurance*. Their goal was to achieve a crossing of the entire mass of Antarctica from sea to sea, passing through the South Pole.

However, before they could actually make land, their ship became trapped in the pack ice. The expedition party watched helplessly as meticulously, over time, the *Endurance* was reduced to splinters by the heaving mass of ice. Shackleton guided the full crew onto the ice, and what followed is one of the great survival stories of human history.

For the next two years they survived by sledging their way along the treacherous ice packs of Antarctica. At times melting ice beneath their feet threatened to cast them into the sea. At other times they faced cold of a kind almost no one survives. But survive they did, for twenty-four months. And eventually Shackleton guided them to a small island from which he and a handful of the men piled into one of the tiny wooden boats they'd salvaged, launching out across the most formidable stretch of open ocean on the planet. Then, largely without navigational aid, Shackleton threaded a needle that was still lost in a haystack, landing the small crew and their dingy on desolate South Georgia Island.

Shackleton then tirelessly persisted with a new crew and ship until he was able to return to the tiny island where the remainder of his men held out. After two years on Antarctica—by the rest of the world presumed dead—Shackleton brought every man under his charge through to safety.

Every man made it *home.*

Will you? Will I?

Not in our own strength, wisdom, or righteousness. But there stands one last great He-is-able-promise.

> Now to him who is able to keep you from stumbling and to present you blameless before the presence of his glory with great joy, to the only God, our Savior, through Jesus Christ our Lord, be glory, majesty, dominion, and authority, before all time and now and forever. Amen. (Jude 1:24–25)

This great promise was first written to believers experiencing incredible pressures from a godless society, a compromising church, and their own wavering inner resolve.

The Holy Spirit calls you to look one more time at what God can do for you. Quite simply, God can keep you from falling and never making it home.

42

WATCH YOUR STEP!

Here's some great news. God "is able to keep you from stumbling" (Jude 1:24).

Sounds great! But what does that mean, exactly?

As always it is imperative that we check the context to see what Jude meant as the Holy Spirit guided him to write these words.

Read through Jude's brief letter, and you'll discover that by "stumbling" he is not referring to losing the salvation God has given to you as a gift by His grace. Rather he is referring to falling prey to the many dangers of which he warns in this letter. These dangers primarily have to do with compromise in our walk with Christ. They include

- "Christians" urging that you lighten up on your moral convictions (v. 4),
- being less than upright in sexual matters (v. 4),
- minimizing Jesus' sovereign authority and lordship (v. 4),
- despising leadership and authority (vv. 6–8),
- displaying destructive sins of speech (v. 10),
- interpreting and living life self-centeredly (v. 12),
- grumbling and complaining (v. 16),

- being arrogant (v. 16), and
- proceeding through life by earthly, human wisdom (vv. 18–19).

God is able to keep you from such things.

In your Bible you'll probably spot the same English word "keep" or "kept" in verses 1, 6 and 21, but those instances translate a different Greek word. In each of those places, the word means to protect something by watching over it.[1] Thus Jude writes to those being "kept for Jesus Christ" (1:1). That is to say, God is watching over them for Jesus' sake.

Interestingly, God then, at the close of the letter, commanded, "Keep yourselves in the love of God" (v. 21).

Wait! Which is it? Am I kept by God, or do I keep myself? And besides, I thought we already settled this—I can't. Only God can.

You're right about that part. But remember, this particular Greek word has the idea of "watching over." So God is calling you to keep watch over your life, but He is not placing upon you the ultimate responsibility to get yourself home.

He promises He alone can and will get you home (v. 24). The Greek word used here describes guarding or protecting something that "*has been entrusted* so that it is not lost or damaged."[2] It pictures God keeping us as His own by posting a guard around us.[3]

So God watches over you (v. 1), and He calls you to join Him in doing so (v. 21), but He does more than just watch over you. He actively guards, shields, and protects you.

How does God do that?

Directly and personally, yes. But He does so also by the use of certain means. God does it, but He often does so via His own appointed means. In this case that includes your cooperation—watching or keeping vigilant in spiritual things.

Thus Jude writes, "But you, beloved, building yourselves up in your most holy faith and praying in the Holy Spirit, keep yourselves in the love of God, waiting for the mercy of our Lord Jesus Christ that leads to eternal life" (vv. 20–21).

God does the keeping, but He works through your obedience in building yourself up in faith, praying in the Holy Spirit, and consciously walking under the banner of His love.

Peter said much the same thing in his second letter. In fact he too spoke of making sure we "will never fall" (2 Peter 1:10). Now read the run-up to that statement and see how God intends to makes sure that never happens.

> His divine power has granted to us all things that pertain to life and godliness, through the knowledge of him who called us to his own glory and excellence, by which he has granted to us his precious and very great promises, so that through them you may become partakers of the divine nature, having escaped from the corruption that is in the world because of sinful desire. [So far this is all God!] For this very reason, make every effort [now God begins to tell us how He is going to accomplish all this] to supplement your faith with virtue, and virtue with knowledge, and knowledge with self-control, and self-control with steadfastness, and steadfastness with godliness, and godliness with brotherly affection, and brotherly affection with love. For if these qualities are yours and are increasing, they keep you from being ineffective or unfruitful in the knowledge of our Lord Jesus Christ. For whoever lacks these qualities is so nearsighted that he is blind, having forgotten that he was cleansed from his former sins. Therefore, brothers, be all the more diligent to confirm your calling and election, for if you practice these qualities you will never fall. (2 Peter 1:3–10)

Did you see that? "You will never *fall*." Jude uses a derivative of that same word in telling us what God is able and willing and committed to doing in your life (1:24).

God will keep you. It is His job, one that only He can perform. And as the one in charge, He determines that He will do it in and through your steps of obedience. He is working in you to enable you even in those (Phil. 2:12–13). God will keep you. When you are kept, it will be God who does it, but He won't do it apart from your obedience.

Not only can God keep you from falling, but God can make you stand in His glorious presence—"to present you" (Jude 1:24).

That may not sound like much to you at the moment, but consider just what that means. When someone was made to "stand," it described a formal presentation of someone of lower rank to another of higher rank, thus making him have a rightful standing in the presence of that exalted one.

When someone is brought into the presence of the Queen of England, her servants carefully prepare the individual, schooling him on proper protocols and etiquette. They then usher him into her presence, giving him a rightful audience with the queen.

God has done this for you through Jesus Christ. "Through [Jesus] we have also obtained access by faith into this grace *in which we stand*" (Rom. 5:2). As a follower of Jesus Christ you have been given as a gift ("grace") the right (by way of God's declaration that Christ's righteousness be counted as yours, "justified," v. 1) to stand in the presence of God as His very own child.

What a gift! Furthermore, God assures you that He is able to keep you in this standing right up to the final day, when you are ushered before His throne.

Consider how infinitely more amazing this is than having been given a standing and audience with any earthly queen or king!

Three times the Bible tells us "our God is a consuming fire" (Heb. 12:29; Deut. 4:24; 9:3). To stand in God's presence is to be consumed. Yet, by His grace, we are not consumed. God gives us a standing in His own glorious, holy presence!

On Saturday night, August 21, 2004, Jose Webster, age thirty-six, led his longtime girlfriend Karla Ramos, age twenty-six, and their four children to the Summit Heat Treating Plant in Akron, Ohio, where he worked. Though events remain sketchy, Jose apparently strangled Karla before the eyes of their children, threw her body into the furnace, and climbed in over top of her in an inexplicable and horrifying murder-suicide.[4]

No one can survive such intense heat. Jose was counting on it.

Do you understand that while we were in full, suicidal flight from God's authority, Jesus Christ came and took upon Himself the flaming judgment of God's just wrath against our sin? And having satisfied the holiness and wrath of God against us, Jesus' own righteous standing is counted to us, so that we can stand in His Father's presence—accepted, loved, embraced, and welcomed.

43

BLAMELESS AND JOYFUL

Not only does God make you to stand before Himself justified, welcomed, and accepted, but He also guarantees your posture there will have two distinct markers about it. One reveals that which *will not be* true of you on that great day, and the other what *will be* true.

First, God keeps you and makes you to stand before His own presence *without fault.* God is able "to present you blameless before the presence of his glory" (Jude 1:24).

By "blameless" He does not mean *perfect.* It is not that you'll pass throughout life without ever doing anything worthy of blame before an infinitely holy God. Solomon—and they don't get any wiser than he—said, "Surely there is not a righteous man on earth who does good and never sins" (Eccl. 7:20). No, we all sin, and we all fall short of the measuring stick of God's own glory (Rom. 3:23).

So how is God going to present us in His own holy presence without blame?

By transference.

God transferred all your blame, guilt, culpability, and responsibility for your sins to Jesus when He was on the cross. There "the LORD . . . laid on him the iniquity of us all" (Isa. 53:6). "He himself bore our sins in his body on the tree" (1 Peter 2:24).

Therefore, when the ledger of heaven is opened to the entry with your name upon it, there will be nothing there for which you can be blamed. You will be rendered blame*less*. And this "in the presence of his glory" (Jude 1:24)! Under the brightest light, you will come through without any accusation.

But, if you dare to believe it, the news gets even better. That tells you what will not be true of you at that great assize. Yet there will be something else just as wonderful on that day. You will stand before the very throne of God under the white-hot light of His emanating glory "with great joy" (v. 24)!

Ponder that for a moment.

How could that *ever* be?

Everything you are worried the guy next to you will find out, everything you're worried about being broadcast, made known, and unveiled to the world—gone! Every skeleton in your closet, the past you're worried will catch up with you, every sin, failure, blemish, and imperfection will be absent. It just won't be there.

In their place will be the eternal, perfect righteousness of Jesus Christ Himself, having been put to your account and counted as your very own by God the Father.

As relieved as you'll be over what is not there, your breath will be taken away by what is there.

You'll discover that God was serious when He said that by His decree you have "become the righteousness of God" (2 Cor. 5:21) by virtue of His divine grace.

Justified—that's the great theological word. Maybe you've heard the old Sunday school definition for justification: Just as if you'd never sinned. It's true, but it's insufficient. In fact, it is *way* better than that! Jerry Bridges says that to be justified is to be treated just as if you had always *obeyed*.[1]

Oh my!

But isn't that what Jesus did? He always obeyed. Not only did Jesus not sin, but He also always and in every moment and in each circumstance fulfilled all the righteousness requirements of God.

God has decided that all who repent and believe in Christ will be given His Son's standing in His presence.

Can you imagine traveling into the center of the sun and surviving? The temperature at the core of the sun is approximately 27,000,000 degrees Fahrenheit. Not much survives there.

Remember, this is no mere comparison. The Creator is always greater than the creation. If God created the sun, then God is greater than the sun! 27,000,000 degrees Fahrenheit is hot beyond all comprehension, but it remains nevertheless a finite temperature. God is infinite—an infinite "consuming fire."

Little wonder that the apostle John fell down as a dead man when brought into His presence (Rev. 1:17). You can understand why Isaiah cried, "Woe is me, for I am ruined!" when confronted with God's holy presence (Isa. 6:5, NASB). Ezekiel was allowed to behold the glory of the Lord . . . and fell on his face (Ezek. 1:28; 3:23). Daniel was as holy a man as has ever lived, but he was terrified and fell prostrate before God's presence (Dan. 8:17).

But when ultimately *you* arrive in God's presence, it will be with "great joy"!

Speaking of Daniel, do you remember his three friends who were thrown into the fiery furnace of King Nebuchadnezzar because they refused to worship his image? The flames were so hot that the men who led them to the furnace door fell down dead (Dan. 3:22). Yet "the fire had not . . . any power over the bodies of those men." Indeed "the hair of their heads was not singed, their cloaks were not harmed, and no smell of fire" clung to them (v. 27).

How could this be?

In Nebuchadnezzar's own words, it was because "four men" (not just the three) "were walking in the midst of the fire, and they [were] not hurt" (v. 25). That fourth, mysterious figure "is like a son of the gods," Nebuchadnezzar said.

They survived Nebuchadnezzar's fabulously hot, though finite, fire because God Himself shielded them from its heat. We will survive the heat of God's holy wrath and find welcome instead because God Himself, in Jesus Christ, took that fiery wrath upon Himself in our place.

Instead of being consumed on that day, we have the promise that God "will transform our lowly body to be like his glorious body" (Phil. 3:21).

It's not that He's going to insulate us and protect us from His burning glory but that He will transform us into the same glory! We will burn with His glory from within, yet not be consumed.

God is able to keep you and make sure you stand in His presence without blame and with joy unspeakable.

44

BOTH ABLE *AND* WILLING

Does all this seem just too good to be true? Maybe you wonder, "I know God is *able* to accomplish this, but how do I know He *will*?"

Honest question. Notice Jude's candid answer.

God is able *and* willing to do this for you for six reasons. But before we begin examining them, recognize that we are taking up the language of worship. We must be careful not to destroy the rose by dissecting it. But take it apart we must, for this tells us why God is able to keep His great promises to us.

God is committed to getting you home because *it is His prerogative to do so*. He is "the *only* God." He is unique. There is no other.

Through Isaiah God rightly claims

> I am the Lord, and there is no other, besides me there is no God; I equip you, though you do not know me, that people may know, from the rising of the sun and from the west, that there is none besides me; I am the Lord, and there is no other. . . . [The peoples of Egypt and Africa] shall follow you; they shall come over in chains and bow down to you. They will plead with you, saying: "Surely God is in you, and there is no other, no god besides him." . . . Declare and present your case; let them take counsel together! Who told this long ago? Who declared it of old? Was it not I, the Lord? And there is no other god besides

> me, a righteous God and a Savior; there is none besides me. Turn to me and be saved, all the ends of the earth! For I am God, and there is no other. (Isa. 45:5–6, 14, 21–22)

There is but one God, eternally existing as Father, Son, and Holy Spirit. He is triune; one, yet three; three, yet one. Mystery indeed!

There is nothing and no one in the universe precisely like God. He is not like anything in His creation. Analogy and comparisons fail in revealing Him completely.

He is the "only God." It is thereby His prerogative to do as He pleases. He possesses the exclusive right to conduct Himself toward His creation in any way He wishes.

In His uniqueness, He can do as He sovereignly wills to do. It was His prerogative for you to hear the gospel, for you to believe it, and for you to be saved thereby. It is also His prerogative to keep you and preserve you in that faith until the day you are home forever with Him.

There is no one who can call God to account. There exists no enemy or witness against you able to successfully threaten your passage through this life and into God's eternal presence in heaven. That includes the Devil himself, who is the accuser of believers (Rev. 12:10). Not your own conscience, not your spouse, your parents, or your kids. It is God's sole, unimpeachable prerogative to shower you with His saving and keeping grace.

God is committed to getting you home because *it is His nature to do so*. He is God, our Savior.

The Bible more often speaks of the Son of God being the Savior, but not infrequently God the Father is also spoken of in this way (Luke 1:47; 1 Tim 1:1; 2:3; 4:10; Titus 1:3; 2:10; 3:4). This is because it is God's eternal nature to be a saving God.

Eternal, you say?

Before anything else was—when there existed nothing but Father, Son, and Holy Spirit—how was His saving nature seen?

It was to be seen in His eternal decree to create a world in which saving would be necessary and in which He could exercise that saving action out of no other compulsion than to simply demonstrate that He is a saving God.

God does not save and keep you because He is cornered into doing so by a creation gone awry. He does not save because of something in you—as if you've earned it or managed to manipulate it out of Him!

There is no reason for God's saving grace other than He is simply being Himself. He desires to display the nature of who He is to the entire created order. And He is, by nature, a God of grace.

Before creation—in advance of time, before space, prior to matter—in an eternal decree, the Father set apart the Son to come and achieve and make actual the salvation that you and I have come to embrace. This is the "grace which was granted us in Christ Jesus *from all eternity*" (2 Tim. 1:9, NASB). "He chose us in him *before the foundation of the world*, that we would be holy and blameless before him" (Eph. 1:4). He acted "in hope of eternal life, which God, who never lies, promised *before the ages began*" (Titus 1:2).

That means you don't have to worry about God changing His mind. He won't rethink His plan or suddenly awake to a better option.

It is the very nature of God to be a Savior. He can be nothing else. Having set His love upon you, He would have to deny Himself if He failed to save you and guard you all the way home to His presence, and that He cannot do (2 Tim. 2:13).

God is committed to getting you home because *it is His glory to do so.* Jude prays that to "the only God, our Savior, through Jesus Christ our Lord, be *glory*" (1:25).

Everything about everything is about the glory of God! From beginning to end, from creation through redemption and on to final consummation—the glory of God is the driving force behind it all. God has determined that it will most glorify Himself to save and keep you. Nothing will dislodge Him from this greatest of all missions—redeeming to Himself a people for His glory.

God does not save and keep you because He is sentimental. It isn't even merely because He is compassionate, kind, and loving. It is for those reasons, but not only for those reasons. God chooses to save you and keep you to demonstrate the greatness of His glory as the supremely compassionate, kind, and loving one. God loves and saves and keeps you because it glorifies Him to do so.

Remember, He sees the end from the beginning (Isa. 46:10). He knew what you would be and do. God did not get into this deal and then say, "Well, that didn't go so well. I'd better do something. I need a new plan!"

This was and is and will ever be *the* divine plan—to glorify Himself by magnifying the greatness of His glory as a giver.

God is more committed to the demonstration of His glory than to any other thing in the universe. This is good news for you and me because He has determined the greatest glory will come to Him when His grace is most magnified in His people.

45

BOTH ABLE *AND* WILLING (CONTINUED)

We have seen that God is both able and willing to get you all the way home to eternity with Him because it is His prerogative, nature, and glory to do so. Now notice that God is committed to getting you home because *it is His will to do so.*

Jude prays that "to the only God, our Savior, through Jesus Christ our Lord, be . . . *majesty*" (1:25).

When we talk of "majesty," we are speaking the language of royalty. We describe that which is regal and magnificent. The term looks to God as Sovereign and King and Ruler.

From the throne of God a decree has come down, and it has your name on it! God ordered, "Arrange the affairs of this world so that through a web of human interactions and individual steps of obedience, the gospel of Jesus Christ comes to (insert your name)!" God's servants went about making sure the will of the King was done. And here you are, reading these lines, observing these truths, confronted with the will of your Sovereign and King—a will that is set toward your eternal keeping and salvation!

His decree has been issued: "What I save, I also keep and preserve to the end!"

Remember, God uses means to keep us. None of this is to relieve us of our responsibility to "keep [ourselves] in the love of God" (1:21). It simply means that if you hear that call—the summons of your Lord and King—then through the means of the Word of God, prayer, fellowship, and your obedience, a royal decree is fulfilled in your experience.

God is committed to getting you home because *it is within His power to do so*. Jude prays that "to the only God, our Savior, through Jesus Christ our Lord, be . . . dominion" (1:25).

The Greek word behind "dominion" is more often translated "power." As the sovereign King of all things, God has the raw power to make certain nothing gets between you and eternity with Him. That is to say, He exercises dominion over all that might ever threaten your standing as His own.

Jesus said, "I give them eternal life, and they will never perish, and no one will snatch them out of my hand" (John 10:28). It is "by God's power [that we] are being guarded through faith for a salvation ready to be revealed in the last time" (1 Peter 1:5). Paul could confidently tell his fellow believers, "I am sure of this, that he who began a good work in you will bring it to completion at the day of Jesus Christ" (Phil. 1:6). There is, then, that magisterial statement of the apostle Paul on these matters.

> If God is for us, who can be against us? . . . Who shall separate us from the love of Christ? Shall tribulation, or distress, or persecution, or famine, or nakedness, or danger, or sword? . . . No, in all these things we are more than conquerors through him who loved us. For I am sure that neither death nor life, nor angels nor rulers, nor things present nor things to come, nor powers, nor height nor depth, nor anything else in all creation, will be able to separate us from the love of God in Christ Jesus our Lord. (Rom. 8:31, 35, 37–39)

Did you notice? Nothing "*will be able* to separate us from the love of God." Why is that? Because He *who is able* keeps us!

God is committed to getting you home because *it is His right to do so*. Jude prays, "To the only God, our Savior, through Jesus Christ our Lord, be . . . authority" (1:25).

The word Jude chose here (*exousia*) points to the right to deploy and use power that is available.

The United States military possesses overwhelming power—from handheld weapons to nuclear devices (and others kinds, I am sure, the public knows nothing about). That power can only be released under orders given by those who possess the right to use that power. This is a necessary safety mechanism to make certain that the power is not unleashed needlessly or unwisely. In fact as I type these lines, the president and his people are making a case to the Congress of the United States of America that such authority be granted to strike what they believe to be an offending people.

God, unlike any human being, possesses both the necessary might and the absolute right to use it. He is subject to no one. He seeks permission from no other place, for He alone is God.

He has unilaterally determined to employ the fullness of His might to save you and guide you safely and eternally into His eternal home.

This is overwhelmingly good news!

But it gets better.

Notice the closing words of Jude's great doxology: All this was and is and shall be "before all time and now and forever" (1:25). All of this—God's prerogative, nature, glory, will, power, and right—were settled in Christ by the decree of the Father from all of eternity. Glory of all glories! He has settled all this upon you for your eternal good!

Can I get someone to echo Jude's final amen?

So here is the great news in a nutshell: God's ability to keep you in *the present* is rooted in His choosing of you in *eternity past* and is guaranteed by His ownership of *eternity future.*

In eternity past God exercised His prerogative, demonstrated His nature, determined to show forth His glory, made it His sovereign choice, set in motion His power, and exercised His right to choose you as the object of His eternal love and good will.

In the present God is actively exercising His prerogative, demonstrating His nature, showing forth His glory, sovereignly choosing to demonstrate His great power, as is His right to do, in keeping you.

In the future God will continue to exercise His prerogative, demonstrate His nature, ever increasingly show forth His glory, and continue sovereignly choosing to exercise His right to demonstrate His power on your behalf.

We began by asking, "Do you ever wonder if you're going to make it?"

We all do. But the answer is "Rest assured, you're going to make it all the way home to heaven!"

That's not because of something inside of you but because of all that is within God.

Clearly, *you* can't.

I know *I* can't!
But *God can*! And He has determined that He will.
So, rest. Be at peace.

EPILOGUE

MY DELIGHT

I wonder if you have noticed? A strange exchange has taken place along this journey of ours. Things are not as they were when we began.

My *dilemma* has become my *delight*.

I can't has become *God can!*

His life has become my life.

Because God is able, I am now able . . . not just to read the great apostle's lines, but to make them my testimony: It is not "I, but Christ"!

How has this come to be?

Via a decree issued from the throne of God. By grace. Through Jesus Christ. Through the working of the Holy Spirit.

It is a great mercy.

Why has this come to pass?

For the glory of God. To demonstrate the greatness of His glory as a giver and lover.

That you might love the God who created and redeemed you. That you might live in the love He set upon you in eternity past, that He worked out in time and space, and that He has pledged to you for eternity future. That you might love Him who so loves you. That in His name and by His indwelling ability you might love the others whom He loves.

That the world might get His grace and that God might get His glory.

The dilemma of *I can't,* when viewed through the prism of *God can,* begins to look strangely like a delight—one more wonderful than I ever imagined possible. In that moment my dilemma not only becomes my delight, it is swallowed up by the delight of God Himself—Him who is able . . . and desirous . . . and willing . . . and eager to demonstrate in my experience what He alone is able to do.

NOTES

CHAPTER 1

1. *The NET Bible, New English Translation Bible (NET)*. n.p.: Biblical Studies Press, LLC, 1996. BibleWorks, v.9. Note for Matthew 20:22.

CHAPTER 3

1. Major W. Ian Thomas, *The Indwelling Life of Christ* (Colorado Springs: WaterBrook Multnomah, 2006), 31, emphasis original.

CHAPTER 8

1. Ray Ortlund: http://thegospelcoalition.org/blogs/rayortlund/2013/07/19/nothing-more-acceptable-to-the-father/. Slightly updated wording from John Owen, *Works* (Edinburgh, 1980), II:35.

CHAPTER 9

1. Fanny Crosby, "Blessed Assurance," 1873.

CHAPTER 11

1. Timothy Friberg, Barbara Friberg, and Neva F. Miller, *Analytical Lexicon of the Greek New Testament* (Victoria, Canada: Trafford Publishing, 205), 356.

CHAPTER 12

1. Robert Robinson, "Come, Thou Fount of Every Blessing," 1758.
2. Thomas, *The Indwelling Life of Christ*, 31.

CHAPTER 14

1. C.S. Lewis, *Christian Reflections,* (Grand Rapids: Wm. B. Eerdmans Publishing Co., 2014), 16.

CHAPTER 15

1. Harry Verploegh, ed., *Oswald Chambers: The Best From All His Books* (Nashville: Oliver-Nelson Books, 1987), 99.

CHAPTER 17

1. Arnold R. Fleagle and Donald A. Lichi, *Broken Windows of the Soul* (Camp Hill, Pennsylvania: WingSpread Publishers, 2011), 96.

2. Fritz Rienecker, *A Linguistic Key to the Greek New Testament*, Cleon L. Rogers, Jr., ed., (Grand Rapids: Zondervan Publishing House, 1980), 670.

3. Rienecker, 670.

4. Archibald Thomas Robertson, *Word Pictures in the New Testament* (Grand Rapids: Baker Book House, 1960), 5:351.

5. Warren W. Wiersbe, *The Bible Exposition Commentary: New Testament* (Colorado Springs: Victor, 2001), 2:284.

CHAPTER 18

1. C.S. Lewis, *Mere Christianity* (New York: HarperCollins, 1952), 143.

2. Rienecker, 671.

CHAPTER 20

1. https://crustore.org/four-laws-english/

2. *Oswald Chambers: The Best From All His Books*, ed., Harry Verploegh (Nashville: Oliver Nelson, 1987), 2.

CHAPTER 21

1. "Local History: Surprising discoveries made in 1980 search of reclusive woman's home," *Akron Beacon Journal*, August 4, 2013, https://www.ohio.com/akron/lifestyle/local-history-surprising-discoveries-made-in-1980-search-of-reclusive-woman-s-home.

2. "Local History"

3. "Local History"

4. "Local History"

5. Charles Wesley, "Faith, Mighty Faith," nd.

CHAPTER 22

1. Jerry Wiles, *The Faithful Witness* (Houston: Halcyon Press, 2001), xiv.

CHAPTER 24

1. Miles J. Standford, *The Complete Green Letters* (Grand Rapids: Zondervan, 1983), 3.

2. Standford, 3–4.

3. Standford, 4.

4. Charles Wesley, "Faith, Mighty Faith," nd.

CHAPTER 25

1. https://www.spurgeon.org/resource-library/sermons/order-and-argument-in-prayer#flipbook/

2. Wesley.

CHAPTER 27

1. Erwin W. Lutzer, *Your Eternal Reward* (Chicago: Moody Press, 2015), 31.

CHAPTER 28

1. Lutzer, 107.
2. Lutzer, 107.

CHAPTER 30

1. I offer this story not to argue for the "Faith Promise" system of giving, but as an example of how God provides when His people trust Him to make them a channel for His resources.
2. This story has been adapted from the author's article "Putting Faith Back in the Promise," *Alliance Life*, December 4, 1996. Used with permission.

CHAPTER 31

1. Charles Wesley, "Love Divine, All Loves Excelling," 1747.

CHAPTER 32

1. R.C. H. Lenski, *The Interpretation of St. Paul's Epistles to the Galatians, to the Ephesians and Philippians* (Minneapolis: Augsburg Publishing House, 1961), 499.
2. Wiles, xiv.
3. Warren W. Wiersbe, *Bible Exposition Commentary*: New Testament (Colorado Springs: Victor, 2001), 2:642.
4. I heard Mr. McQuilkin say this in a radio broadcast of WMHK in Columbia, SC in the mid-1980s.

CHAPTER 34

1. Taken from an undated communique from Dr. David Rambo to the official workers of The Christian and Missionary Alliance.
2. G. H. P. Thompson, *The Letters of Paul to the Ephesians, to the Colossians and to Philemon* (Cambridge: University Press, 1967), p.60.

CHAPTER 35

1. A.W. Tozer, *I Call it Heresy* (Harrisburg, Pennsylvania: Christian Publications, 1974), 43.
2. Philip Yancey, *Disappointment With God* (Grand Rapids: Zondervan, 1988), 1.

CHAPTER 36

1. https://abcnews.go.com/WNN/video/school-clerk-helps-suspect-put-weapons-surrender-20020439.
2. David W. Whittle, "I Know Whom I Have Believed," 1883.

3. https://www.theblaze.com/news/2013/08/24/islamic-extremists-slit-throats-of-44-villagers-gouge-out-eyes-of-surviving-victims.
4. Whittle.

CHAPTER 37

1. William D. Mounce, *Word Biblical Commentary: Pastoral Epistles* (Nashville: Thomas Nelson Publishers, 2000), 46:487.

CHAPTER 38

1. Walter Bauer, *A Greek-English Lexicon of the New Testament and Other Early Christian Literature*, ed. Frederick W. Danker, 3rd ed. (Chicago: University of Chicago Press, 2000), BibleWorks. v.9. #5754.4.
2. Mounce, 46:32, 486.

CHAPTER 39

1. The NASB and KJV follow this line of thought.

CHAPTER 40

1. http://www.desiringgod.org/sermons/called-to-suffer-and-rejoice-to-finish-the-aim-of-christs-afflictions
2. Joni Eareckson Tada, *A Place for Healing: Wrestling with the Mysteries of Suffering, Pain, and God's Sovereignty* (Colorado Springs: David C. Cook, 2010), 224.
3. Tada, 224.
4. Tada, 226.
5. Tada, 227–28.

CHAPTER 42

1. Walter Bauer, *A Greek-English Lexicon of the New Testament and Other Early Christian Literature*, ed. Frederick W. Danker, 3rd ed. (Chicago: University of Chicago Press, 2000), BibleWorks. v.9. #7356
2. Bauer, #7842; emphasis original.
3. John MacArthur, *MacArthur New Testament Commentary—2 Peter & Jude*. (Chicago: Moody Press, 2005), WORD*search* CROSS e-book, 20.
4. https://www.upi.com/Police-probe-incinerator-murder-suicide/80981093283988/

CHAPTER 43

1. Jerry Bridges and Bob Bevington, *The Bookends of the Christian Life* (Wheaton: Crossway, 2013), 26.